The
REAL RIDE

To Nan,

Horseback buddies!

Lisa

10-29-18

The
REAL RIDE

My Horseback Journey
From Turmoil to Peace
And Power

By

Lisa Worrell-Whittle

Published by
Mark of Design, LLC
Hillsville, Virginia

Paperback ISBN 978-0-578-20889-3
eBook ISBN 978-0-578-20888-6

Cover Design: Lisa W. Whittle
Front Cover Photo: Lisa W. Whittle
Back Cover Photo: Lisa W. Whittle
Interior Design: Lisa W. Whittle

Printed in the United States of America
Launch Edition September 2018

Www.markofdesignllc.com

Dedication

I would like to dedicate this book to anyone who has loved and lost and needs the inspiration to live and love again.

"Perfection is frustratingly unobtainable,
so, strive to do the best you can."

Lisa

Table of Contents

Foreword

The Real Ride by Lisa Worrell-Whittle is a real ride indeed! If you are human, if you value victory through loss, joy over disappointment, love beyond betrayal, forgiveness over anger, this book will not disappoint! This is a remarkable journey into the world of one remarkable woman: a horsewoman, an entrepreneur, artist, the granddaughter of a beloved pastor, a daughter/wife/mother/ friend. Her story is direct and personal.

Born and raised in a small town in Virginia, Lisa has what my grandmother called "pluck." She does not shy away from living, not from life's challenges, heartaches or hard work. She is always getting back up and in the saddle with true female grit, humor, and love.

Lisa weaves her life story from the present to the past and back again, always tying her life lessons together in a humorous knot of love. You will feel like she is sharing her wisdom from across the kitchen table. Within the first chapter, the ride begins with a triumphant win with her champion horse Mark, then Lisa witnesses his tragic death just days before she closed the deal to sell her trophy-winning stallion. It was a sale which would set her up financially for the rest of her life. Lisa and Mark had a remarkable ride in which Lisa solidly established herself as a high-quality horsewoman. She was 100% devoted to Mark, and if you have ever loved an animal, it is easy to imagine the intense love Lisa felt for her beautiful horse. Her raw pain will break your heart wide open.

After the rough ride of Mark's death, her journey weaves back to a tragic event in her twenties and through more recent struggles. You will join her on the ride of relationships: mother to daughter, husband to wife, friend to friend, church to true fellowship. We witness love and loss, betrayal and forgiveness, distrust restored to trust and on to self-empowerment. In all her relationships, you get to know a champion and a woman of passion with tremendous humor. You will wish to be her friend.

Patricia Joyce Alvord, Cleveland, OH, www.portraitsbypatjoyce.com

Preface

This story started as a movie idea before the traumatic death of my career horse as there were so many twists and turns beginning with the potential sale. I thought the movie would end with the new buyers winning a World Championship, and I would have a large sum of money and frozen semen to boot. It was as close as I had ever come to having my cake and eating it too. At that point, never in my wildest dreams would the story end with the death of my beloved horse. Nor did I have any idea what events would follow or reveal.

Life is full of surprises.

Where I thought I was going each time was different from where I ended up. How stupid could I have been to think money would solve all my problems? I had no idea the real ride had just started. Life is like riding a horse, a Saddlebred horse. Up, down, up, down, up, down. It was a rough ride until I got the hang of it. It took a lot of time before I could get started writing this book. I had a lot of healing and soul-searching to do.

The process of writing this book has brought a lot of healing. I have done the best I can to bring you my story and share many valuable lessons.

One surprising and very important twist within my story is the illustration of why the school shooters shoot.

I have broken a self-publishing cardinal rule of don't use friends and English teachers to edit your book. Without them, I don't think I would have ever made it through this project. Their questions to bring more clarity to the readers made me find answers within myself. The editing process was harder than the initial writing. The real process was in healing, and I have learned to write along the way.

One retired English teacher played a part in the story. Another retired teacher guided me through many tears and frustrations to help in this project. Two others were irreplaceable in the process, along with several other supporting friends with their reader's viewpoints. We all have done the best we can, and I don't begin to claim my book is perfect.

Now, my English teacher editors think they have succeeded in teaching this hillbilly country girl to carefully choose her words, and not to get them twisted. Thank God, they have finally left me to my own devices. I'm having so much fun playing with words I have just simply worn out all my editors. After all, they are retired. Anyone who has ever worked with me knows I have fun when I'm working. They also know, when I'm thinking, it's dangerous for everyone, because I am creative in more things to do and that includes work. Everyone around has tried to keep me running in circles and finally, all my family and friends have given up. I guess I have more heart. I win.

Life is not perfect, people are not perfect, relationships are not perfect. Nothing is perfect. Sometimes we cry, and yet why not laugh.

Some of the thoughts I put on paper may be a surprise to some people, others have experienced the same path. I mean no harm, I have been creative in good humor.

The people participating in this story have known me through various stages of my life, and we have had many life experiences bringing my story to you. If you get half as much out of this book as we have, it will be worthwhile.

Welcome to The Real Ride and enjoy the telling of my journey while I am moving on and breaking new ground.

Acknowledgments

I would like to thank my husband, Tom,
for his encouragement in the writing of this book.
And to everyone who was involved in this story, I couldn't have told
it without you. I offer you a humble thank you.

Introduction

The tragic death of my career horse was a major turning point in my life. In the first chapter, I was catapulted into my grief. I have done my best to capture the feeling of the shock. I thought everything was good and normal until the event made me take a good long look in the mirror. The entire episode put an end to my life as I knew it.

This is my journey to God and self. You may feel thrown from my horse, along with me, into the dust. Out of the confusion, many questions arise. I ride forward in search of many answers as life's reflection peels back layer after layer of myself. Several broken hearts are suffered while persevering to my destination of peace. The trail winds through grief, sadness, frustration, anger, happiness, joy and laughter. My story is horrifying at times and delightfully humorous at others. Experience restful stops along the way in the warm anointment of peace and cool breezes of freedom with storytelling of universal themes and truths. But I will warn you, my journey is not for the faint of heart.

Should you decide you have enough heart to read along, thank you. If my story hits home in your life, skip over what is too hard and continue for the good lessons and humor. I hope you enjoy my illustrations of how crazy life can be and discover something wonderful within these pages.

The
REAL RIDE

I

My Devastating Fall

1

My Horse

Mark of Design, a stallion, and I gave our best performance at the Roanoke Valley Horse Show in Roanoke, Virginia. Our love affair was on display. Together, 'Mark' and I, were music in motion. It was one of the most satisfying rides I ever had with my beautiful stallion and we won the class. The crowd cheered!

My niece was off from school and she was my capable assistant. We stayed with my uncle who lives in town, and my son and husband joined us. My uncle loved eating hotdogs at the show, and he ate two hotdogs the first night Mark and I won. If there was any way he could contribute to another win, it was to keep his winning combination. The next time we showed, my uncle ate two hotdogs.

Saturday night, Mark and I gave a command performance and won the Amateur Five Gaited Championship. We had a perfect ride, and so many of my friends were there supporting us to win. Stallions can be potentially be very hard to handle and sometimes dangerously unpredictable. Most are castrated for safety to handlers. So one little woman and one stallion together was thrilling by itself. On our victory pass, the announcer revved up the crowd by asking for even more applause. I rode by one side of the Coliseum as the applause of the audience competed against the applause of the other side as I rode by their side. The roar of the crowd was the greatest thrill to Mark and me. There was nothing like the adrenaline rush of achieving the win, not to mention overcoming challenging odds. The roar from the applause was the icing on the cake. Those kinds of thrilling highs didn't last for minutes; they lasted for days. The euphoria from achieving the hard-earned goal was worth all the blood, sweat and tears the challenge demanded! Was this a once in a lifetime experience? It was awesome!

In addition to the thrill, earlier on the same evening, Mark's first offspring, My Lovely Lady, won the Open Fine Harness Championship. A few nights before, she had won the Junior Fine Harness division. She was becoming a magnificent show horse in her own right. The mare was such a diva when entering the gate, her showing was as if she owned the world! She loved being in the ring, as she was a show horse through and through. Her wins only added to Mark's achievement as it proved he could sire top show horses.

I walked into the Coliseum to buy a refreshing drink, and a little girl tugged on my riding coat.

"Were you that lady who rode that beautiful horse? she asked.

"That could be you. Have you ever ridden a Saddlebred? I said with a smile. "Ask your mom to let you give horseback riding a try," I coached. I felt like for the first time, I was able to represent a breed I love to the public. Everything about my show at Roanoke was thrilling. Thirty-five years earlier at that same show was the most beautiful Saddlebred I had ever seen, My Lovely. When I went shopping for broodmares, I was ecstatic when I had the opportunity to buy a daughter out of the very same lovely mare. I can still picture that beautiful mare showing.

Mark was a grandson of my vision. It was a fitting place to have our best show ever. I named his first offspring after his grand dam or maternal grandmother, My Lovely Lady; the likeness was striking.

After our first win at this show, I was approached by a potential buyer asking if Mark was for sale. I knew they had more resources to take Mark all the way to a World Championship title. No one makes it to the top by themselves, and my funds and team support were limited. His new home would be just over an hour away, and I could sit in the stands and watch his career continue. I was interested in what they could offer my grand horse.

Mark was impressive both times they watched his show, and the deal was materializing. The agent and buyer wanted to see Mark compete again at the next show. In a couple of weeks, I packed up my stallion, his daughter, and my niece and planned for another excellent performance. I was horrified when I realized I couldn't hear the classes called from where we were stabled. We were ready and waiting for our class, taking into account putting on the bridle and my coat. I tried my best to have enough help to overcome the impending disaster, but my backup communication method broke down, and we were rushed to get to the class on time. Mark's warm-up was cut short, and he didn't like to be rushed. Our performance suffered, and it killed the deal. The largest possible sale I ever had just went POOF. It seemed no matter how much I did; it was never enough. I can't explain how upset I was over my misfortune.

I still had to compete in more classes at this show with Mark and his daughter, and I sought out the show manager. I explained my problem not being able to hear the classes called and suggested a texting system in addition to the public announcing system. The show manager was at the entrance gate, and she volunteered to text me, so I could make my classes. My Lovely Lady made a fantastic show to be the Reserve Champion on the Junior Fine Harness class, and Mark gave a much better performance and tied next to the current World Champion and two other Champion Title holding horses. But the damage to the potential sale had already been done.

I was so disheartened from not having enough help for a successful show, I was beaten. I decided not to go to the World Championship. I felt I couldn't provide Mark with a real shot at the title he deserved, without a familiar team supporting us. No one makes it to the top by themselves.

Defeated like I had not known before, I came home with anger seeping out like I had not met before. The two little words, "I quit," was an unknown combination to me until now. I snapped at my husband while fixing the kitchen sink faucet. I didn't have the patience to work with tools. I was usually the fix-it person. When I stepped out of the car after riding with him to buy new hardware, I verbally bit his head off.

"Well, how does it feel to ride with someone growling and b**ching?" as I slammed the door. I gave him a mirror to what he had done to me many times in the past. "It's no fun is it? I can't even stand MYSELF!" I snapped. What has happened? Who am I?

In another month, my intention with the next show was just to have fun again. I had no help at all at this show, and my stallion and I went alone. But fellow horse people and trainers noticed we were alone and offered their help. A Mexican offered to help braid the ribbon in Mark's mane, and I accepted and was grateful. I asked a friend to help brace Mark's tail. She helped me mount and helped a few minutes in the warm-up ring before she left to get her horses ready. Mark's training strap came loose on the far end of the warm-up ring, and another horsewoman stepped in to help. I went on into the show ring, and in a few passes, Mark cast a shoe. I rode up to the ringmaster, and he asked if I had help.

"No," I said.

Two farriers came in ribbing each other that they were going to help me. So often they treated me like I was one of them because they approved of my farrier work. The shoe was back on, and the farriers offered me a leg up. It was far from a graceful mount in the middle of the show ring, and we all laughed. I felt like an orphan, but friends made my show fun. Mark's performance made the sale a possibility again, and the agent wanted a tryout.

In all our show career, Mark had always been paying attention to only me in the warm-up ring until the previous show, and he began to look around at all other horses there. Maybe it was time to pick his direction, a breeding horse or a show horse? He was such a blast to show. It was my fateful decision to castrate my horse. Since I had a tank full of frozen semen, he could still sire foals. He was possibly going to be sold to a juvenile rider, and the rulebook didn't allow minors to show a stallion. If this buyer didn't want him, I knew someone else would. My husband and I had processed the frozen semen ourselves. He was completely familiar with laboratory procedures and I could deal with everything concerning the horse. With the semen as an asset, I decided to have my vet castrate my horse before I gave the agent a tryout.

In the next three months, my vet performed the castration, healing moved forward, the deal moved to a tryout, the tryout was successful, the deal was struck, the pre-purchase exam was completed, and that was the beginning of the most stress I had ever been under in my life.

Two months had gone by after the pre-purchase exam, and I was weary from the eight-month business deal that seemed would never end. That Thursday morning, I hauled Mark over to my veterinarian's clinic for possible exploratory surgery to find the cause of yet another infection. I unloaded Mark from the trailer and led my beloved horse into the clinic. He stood patiently beside me while I sat and watched my vet impatiently pace back and forth, waiting for his partner to come. As time went by, my vet became more impatient, still pacing back and forth, mumbling out loud, "come on, come on." Mark eased over to me and put his lips down on the back of my hand, took his teeth and intentionally pinched my skin. I was quite irritated with him at the time, but looking back, he was telling me he didn't want to be there. I wish I had listened.

The partner finally came, and I felt the tension in their discussion. My vet wanted to do the surgery, but his partner didn't want to. I remembered her saying if she did surgery on every little infection following previous surgeries, that would be all she would be doing. Apparently, with animal surgery, infection was a common occurrence. Had I known what I know now, I would have paid a lot more attention to what she was saying, but the pressure of the whole ordeal was taking its toll.

We decided to move on with the surgery. I had also been present for the previous two surgeries. I watched my vet sedate Mark and positioned him on a surgical mattress surrounded by all necessary equipment and supplies. As soon as he cut Mark open to inspect for the infection, my heart hit the floor. Something didn't feel right. But I just thought the sale might not happen. I had no idea how wrong things were going to go. My horrible feeling had to be like what a mother had when she knew her missing child was dead before anyone else did. It was a sinking feeling I hope I never again experience. Only a catastrophic, tragic outcome could be the result of such a deep premonition of grief and despair. From that moment, I felt numb.

I left the clinic after the surgery was over. This time, I was glad to leave Mark at the clinic for post-surgery care because I could barely function when I walked out. My numbness, I could not shake. I was confident the vets would care for him. I don't remember what I did for the rest of the day, but I remember quite well, that day was the beginning of months of sleepless nights.

The next morning, I went into the clinic to check on Mark, and the vets were hosing the surgical site with the utmost care anyone could ask. I had kept my composure through months of what seemed to be an unending business deal. I couldn't hold it together anymore, and I finally unloaded to my vet.

"I CAN'T DO THIS ANYMORE! THE AGENT IS MAD AT ME, YOU'RE MAD AT THE AGENT, YOUR PARTNER IS IN A WAD, AND I CAN'T HOLD THIS TOGETHER ANYMORE!"

No one uttered a word and just kept working. I knew I wasn't helping, so I turned and walked out.

Looking back, I felt as if I gave up before Mark did.

I went home to my husband and son and tried to take care of whatever chore was at hand, but my heart and mind were in one place, and my body was in another. We decided to make things easier and go out to get something to eat. It was next to impossible to be present in the moment and carry on any conversation. As soon as we got home, my husband asked me what was wrong, and I told him something didn't feel right about Mark. Maybe I didn't want to sell him after all. Maybe I should keep him, and perhaps I should take my shot at the world championship. I couldn't put my finger on it; just something felt wrong.

Another night, I lay tossing and turning. The next morning it was 9:00 when I heard my phone ring. I got out of bed at that late hour, which was unheard of for me. I found a missed call from my vet.

I called him back and he said, "Lisa, Mark has taken a turn for the worse and you need to take him to Tech." Tech refers to the Maryland/Virginia College of Veterinary Medicine located in Blacksburg, Virginia, approximately one hour away.

"Ok," I said.

I can remember moving in slow motion. It was the strangest thing. I--got--on--my--clothes, --brushed--my--teeth, --put--on--my-- makeup, --and while brushing my hair-- suddenly, it began to compute! Mark has taken a turn for the worse!

Reality kicked me in gear!

I ran through the kitchen, snatched up breakfast and ran through the living room past my husband and said, "MARK HAS TAKEN A TURN FOR THE WORSE, I'VE GOT TO TAKE HIM TO TECH!"

And swoosh! Out the door I went!

Even though it took me a while to get going, I only live a quarter of a mile from the vet clinic. It took ten minutes after the ominous phone call.

As I drove into the vet clinic, I realized my horse trailer was there but not my truck. I jumped out of the car, and my vet was outside the clinic getting something out of his vehicle.

"Can I borrow your truck? It will take me an hour to pick mine up in Hillsville," I said.

"You can borrow my truck, but Mark's not gonna make it," he said.

I couldn't believe what I just heard. I marched past my vet on the way to the stall, and to my shocking surprise, Mark was lying on his side with an IV in his neck, a plastic tube leading to the IV fluid bag hanging from the ceiling. A spray of violent diarrhea was on the wall directly across from the door. I stood horrified in the doorway of the stall watching my horse twitch. My vet entered and stood over my horse while two other vets were standing motionless, an arm's length away.

"WHAT HAPPENED!" I said. I was shocked!

"I, I, I, I've never seen this before! I mean, I have seen this before but never at such great speed! Usually, after violent diarrhea, you have eighteen to twenty-four hours to do something about it! This was FORTY-FIVE MINUTES! At 8:00 he was fine and before 8:30, he was getting a little restless and suddenly he had violent diarrhea!" explained my vet.

"Well, DO SOMETHING!" I demanded!

"He, he, he, he's dead! He's brain dead. HE'S DEAD!" he stuttered.

There was a deafening **silence**... A motionless **shock**...

It was as if a bomb had just exploded and we were numb. A shell shocking event I hope I never experience again.

My husband came and headed straight for Mark's stall. The stall door was on the right, and the main part of the stall was on the left. The stall front hid Mark's lifeless body from my husband's view. I had slumped down in the stall door, and the vets were standing on the opposite side of me. As my husband marched in, looked at me, looked at the vets and continued to approach the stall door. When he saw Mark, his expression turned to horror as he glanced at me and burst into tears. Just when I thought it couldn't get any worse, a grown man sobbing with grief. He turned away, crying out loud, and left.

I have to give my husband credit. It took him five seconds to take in the situation and to cry. It took me five months to be in touch enough with myself to finally let go. He said later, "When I walked in and saw you sitting in the doorway and the three vets just standing there, I couldn't figure out what y'all were doing. Nobody was doing anything or saying anything. When I looked down at that magnificent creature dead on the ground, his feet were showing the new shoes you worked so hard to make; I realized what I was seeing. It was **disbelief.**"

I finally found the strength to get up and walk over to Mark and kneel over him. I wanted to rub him for my last time while he was still warm. As I crouched beside him, my friend Lori from the Wellness Center called. "How's Mark?" she asked.

"**Dead**," I replied.

There was a silence and we both gently hung up. Later, she told me, "For the first time in my life, I wept for someone else."

My vet said he would take Mark anywhere I wanted, and his partner volunteered her graveyard and her dad's backhoe to lay him to rest. I stood up refusing a tear, determined to show strength, in which life goes on, and calmly said, "No." I wanted him buried on the farm with my favorite dog, Buddy and a beloved family horse, Judy.

"You've got Judy?" his partner asked.

I nodded. Judy and I taught his partner to ride when she was a little girl, and in fact, we taught many of my friends to ride. Buddy was an Australian Shepherd and my constant companion for fifteen years. There was no other place Mark could be laid to rest, but home.

"If you would please take off his shoes for me and cut off his tail hair for a switch, and we'll bury him in his blanket and the halter with his nameplate." I said. I walked to my car and drove straight to my farm to await the delivery of my horse.

Life sucked.

II

Surviving the Loss

2

Standing Tall

It was a cold, muddy, overcast day. I was sitting in my car, waiting for my vet to bring Mark's body home as he had promised. Why is it after a death that time just seems to get lost?

While I waited, I picked the gravesite up on a hill, overlooking the pasture where Mark was raised. It was easily visible from the barn where Mark and I had spent most of our time together. I couldn't imagine any other place to lay my horse to rest than the farm where he was born and raised. He was coming home. I sat alone in total numbness. My thoughts were sketchy. How did this happen?

I had just watched the greatest horse in my world die. I thought about the Saddlebred birth rate numbers which had dwindled to less than a thousand per year. Could someday they all be gone?

"Mark, I couldn't save you, but I promise, I will help save the American Saddlebreds." Am I crazy? I just made a promise to a dead horse.

The burial troops began to trickle in. I watched my neighbor, the husband of my vet's partner, carefully dig the grave with his father-in-law's backhoe. The machine was unfortunately used to bury animals of clients who couldn't bear the job on their own.

My vet showed up with Mark's body covered in the back of his pickup. I had asked that Mark be in his favorite blanket with the halter he always wore. The vet had pulled the shoes and handed them over to me so that I could keep a piece in memory of him. He also handed over his tail as I asked for a switch. Maybe someday.

I watched as he drove his truck over the pasture and stopped to contemplate how to get up the slick hillside. My vet made a judgment call, just how hard and fast to attempt the hill for position to easily slip Mark's body in his grave. His calculation was perfect. My vet was still caring for this grand horse even after he was dead. I started to walk over to climb the hill but abruptly did an about-face, not because it was too hard for me, but because I thought it would be a little easier on them if they buried him without me so close. My pain was so intense; I thought everyone could feel it.

I went into the barn and watched the burial process through the office window. My vet's partner was very particular how she placed animals in their graves. She wanted them to look like they were sleeping. I knew what she was talking about because I had done the same thing with the old gray mare, Judy. I knew she would take care to place Mark as if he were sleeping.

When the burial was over, we all met in the parking lot. They wanted me to know they had done their best. I thanked them for the care only neighbors can give in time of real need.

My vet and I were standing shoulder to shoulder. I turned and looked up to him. We both felt responsible for the tragedy that had unfolded. He was a very strong and stout man, and I will never forget the look on his face after he helped to bury my magnificent horse.

"You know--if I had to do it over again--I would still pick you," I whispered.

"Yeah--but this is gonna take me a long time to get over," he said very softly.

As I glanced over at him, I saw he was giving all he had to choke back tears. But oddly enough, when he was feeling so low, as I looked up at him, he looked to be ten foot tall.

I always knew he provided the best care to his patients, because he was the vet who cared the most.

3

The First Week

Everyone had left the farm on that burial day, except for me. Where do I go? And what do I do? I had just got in my car when Lori called. She asked what could she do to help.

"I don't know what to do with myself. Could I just come swimming?" I asked.

"Come on, I'll meet you at the Wellness Center. Who's taking care of the horses tomorrow?" she asked.

"Mmm, uh, oh..." I muttered. That was more than I could deal with at the time.

"I'll take care of the horses until you're ready to come back," she said.

"Thanks," I replied weakly.

I drove to the Wellness Center. The place was empty, and Lori instructed to lock up when I left. What a great friend in time of need. I had helped her with a problem horse, and she had bought a super cute Saddlebred from me.

There is a special bond between horse people.

I put my face down in the water and swam in slow motion. The water felt cool washing away the tears compared to the burn of wiping the them away with my hand. Several times I held onto the edge of the pool to keep from sucking in water as I choked back the tears. The shock from this tragedy lasted days or maybe even weeks. Everything I did was in slow motion. I had no idea how long I was in the pool that day. I crawled out and drove home to yet another sleepless night.

Sunday, I stayed home, and spent another sleepless night trying to figure out what I had done wrong that led to Mark's death. The best thing I did that day was to decide this was going to be a loud recovery. Nothing I felt would be held inside. I desperately wanted to move on and I hated feeling like I did.

Tragic events are giant holes in the road of life. It is useless to try to go around these holes or jump over them. The only way I can get past this misery is to go down as far as necessary, hit bottom, and then climb out. Then I could move on.

This time, I took a swan dive into this grief, hoping to hit bottom as soon as possible. I intended to deal with this tragedy head on. I would do the best I could, but I knew it wasn't going to be easy.

Monday, I decided to go back to the Wellness Center and swim until I couldn't swim anymore, hoping it would help me sleep. I swam two and a half hours on Monday, an hour and a half on Tuesday and another hour and a half on Wednesday. Sleep didn't come. I laid awake all night. In the middle of one night, I got up and found a movie to watch. I fell asleep shortly after it started and woke up just as it ended, so at least, I slept two hours. Trying to figure out what I had done wrong and what I could have done differently just rolled around in my head like a broken record. The sound of the TV stopped the noise in my head. I tried playing soft music to do the same thing. It worked, but after a few nights, the music didn't work at all.

Tuesday, I went to the vet clinic and sat with Angela in her office. I wanted to sit with someone who understood my sorrow. Sometimes I just sat in silence, sometimes I talked about trying to figure out what I had done wrong and sometimes I had what I refer to my daily rant, letting the anger out for losing my horse, my life's work. One day, I was ranting about trying to keep everyone happy, along with the horse deal and surgical procedures.

"But it was YOUR horse." Angela said very kindly.

Why was I trying to please everybody and putting myself last on the list? Was it such a bad thing to be concerned for others? What did I do wrong?

Wednesday when I left her office, I went to the monument company to see about a granite marker for Mark's grave. I looked at a few possibilities, but I walked out unable to make a decision or to spend money I felt like I didn't have.

As I pulled out of the parking lot, I called Angela. "Angela. This is gonna sound like a stupid question, but what day is this?"

"It's Wednesday," she said.

In a few minutes, she sent a text. It pictured a popular cartoon character saying, "If you can laugh in a difficult situation, you win." The message gave a different flavor to the day.

That night, my mom called from Florida where my uncle was visiting her and my stepdad. I had informed them about Mark a few days before. She took her turn at trying to cheer me up with her story. They had gone to the dog races earlier, and my uncle decided to place a $2 bet. The dog came in, and it looked like on the board he had won $26. He went to collect on his bet and the racetrack proceeded to dole out a wad of money.

"Don't you think you made a mistake?" my uncle asked.

"No sir, you won $267, we just couldn't fit all the numbers on the payout board," they replied.

I could hear laughing in the background. I could imagine Mom scrunching her nose up that he won and not her. Sibling rivalry must not ever die; it only takes on a new flavor. I couldn't help but chuckle. He must have eaten two hotdogs. I laughed. I won.

On Thursday morning, after a week of sleepless nights, and miles of swimming, I was exhausted. I knew I was going to get through this and I had decided to spend the day in bed. I physically hurt from head to toe.

My husband, Tom, came in around 9:30. "Are you getting up today?" he asked.

"Look at me. Look at me! I wasn't this upset when my dad died or when my grandparents died. IT'S JUST A HORSE!" I yelled.

I flopped hard back in bed. This was the first time Tom experienced one of my daily rants. He quietly slipped out of the room. In about ten minutes he came back in, walked around to my side of the bed, and very kindly sat down beside me.

"It wasn't just a horse. Parents and grandparents were expected to die, and yours were sick. Mark was a shock. He was everything I've seen you work for since I've known you, the loss of prestige, the potential world title, not to mention the money," he said.

I sat straight up in bed with my eyes wide open.

"You know Tom, you are right. I had worked my way so close to the top that the fall was SHATTERING! You couldn't have beaten me with a stick from head to toe and made me hurt any more than I do already. I think I'm just gonna lay in bed today and rest," I said.

"Ok," he said and left.

I decided to call a friend or two and inform them of my tragic news. One friend I called had begun to feel like a sister. We were about the same age, married with one child, and both of us trained horses. When I started telling her my news, all I could do was babble.

"What, what is this all about?" she said.

"I LOST MARK!" I finally got my news out.

"Oh no... What happened?" she said.

I told her a short version of the story, but basically, my horse was gone. She told me of the year before when they had lost one of their champions and how hard it hit everyone. Wow, I could sure sympathize with that.

"And everyone moped around for about a week," she said.

I thought, "A week.... a week...Here it is a week later, and I don't even want to get out of bed. Yes, you lost a horse, but you have forty more great horses! I don't have forty more good horses, just one and he's gone!"

"I can't even get out of bed," I whined.

"Well maybe that's what you need to do," she said. She was very comforting. She began to end our conversation.

"I gotta go, I've got a sh**ty day. I've got to meet with the accountant, and pack for vacation, and I hate doing that," she said.

We talked a little more, and again she said, "I've got a sh**ty day, I've got to meet with the accountant, pack for vacation. Oh, I've got a sh**ty day."

I thought to myself, "A sh*tty day... A SH**TY DAY...are you kidding me? Didn't you hear me? My world just ended and you're telling me that you are probably making money if you are talking to an accountant, and you're going on vacation with your hot husband, and THAT'S A SH**TY DAY?!"

"Trade ya," I said.

"Teehee" slipped out of her mouth and then a concise, "No."

The phone call ended. I guess I won with the sh**ty day competition. I all but slammed the phone down and thought, "Oh my God, we are way too much like sisters! First, they will be very caring and pick you up when you're down, but as soon as they do, competition starts again! I don't have a sister and WHY ON EARTH WOULD I WANT ONE, if this is what it's like!" For the second time today, I flopped back in bed. I was so upset after that phone call. But then again, I wasn't in very good shape before the phone call.

All day long I could hear her little "Teehee"...."teehee."

I've never been able to lie in bed all day long. I get bored and get up. But today, I broke my record. Not that I want to put it down for posterity, but it happened. By 3:30, I finally got up and went to the kitchen to get something to drink, and my son had gotten home from school.

He took one look at me, and his eyes widened.

"What is wrong with you?!" he asked.

I don't even want to imagine how I looked. "Son, I hope this doesn't happen, but sometime in your life there might be something so awful that happens, you don't want to get out of bed. Today happens to be my day. I'll be alright, but right now, I'm going back to bed," I said.

"Ok," he calmly said.

I finally got up to eat a little supper with my husband. All day long, I heard in my head "Teehee." At this point, I began to chuckle at the whole conversation. I sat down and told Tom the conversation, and at the end, "trade ya!"

"That was quick!" as he snapped to attention in his chair.

Finally, I got a laugh out of my difficult situation. I won.

Friday, I went to the clinic to spend a little time in Angela's office. A phone appointment was planned with the buyer's agent to discuss the details of the press release concerning Mark's death later in the day. As I stepped out of her office to leave, I looked across the clinic at the stall where Mark had died. His splat of diarrhea was still on the wall.

"Can't someone just clean this SH** OFF THE WALL?!" I demanded.

At that very moment, Tammy, from the small animal clinic down the hill, was right in my face, smiling. She was shorter than I was, so I was looking down at this overwhelming beam of sunlight. I almost had to squint my eyes.

"Well, why don't you clean the sh** off the wall?" she teased.

My eyelids fluttered, and my mouth flew open as I heard my last nerve snap. It was beyond being hit with icy cold water when I never even knew it was coming. It took me some time before any words would come out.

"I-- COULD JUST--BREAK-- YOUR NECK!" I strained.

She still didn't grasp the enormity of the situation and came back with something just as inappropriate as before. Angela was standing very close, knowing the situation, she sucked in her breath not knowing what might happen next. Great anger boiled up from the pit of my being.

"The onnnnnnly reason YOU'RE LIVING--is because I'M NOT-- A VIOLENT....PERSON!" I hissed.

I turned to walk to my car, and I can truthfully say I was shaking all over. She was still on my *ss and again followed with another useless comment, and I whirled around.

"ANGELA, DOESN'T SHE KNOW?!" I stammered.

I didn't wait for a reply, but whirled back around, walked to my car, balancing on my shaky, wet noodle legs. I got in my car and tried to calm myself before driving home. I was shaking all over, inside and out. This shaky feeling was not going to leave me anytime soon. It was going to take time before I could land back on earth. Home was only a quarter of a mile away. I left.

Once home, I mustered up the courage to stand up on two legs as shaky as mine. I wanted the comfort of my recliner. I somehow made it and flopped down only to clench each chair arm and try to convince myself to calm down. "Just calm down, just calm down," I kept saying silently to myself. I finally quit shaking. It felt like my brain had just been through a hurricane, and my heart and body were shaken to the core.

Breathing deeply, the calmness was a welcomed friend. I phoned Angela.

"What just happened?" I asked.

"You should have seen your face! In the twenty years, I have known you, I have never heard you threaten bodily harm," she said.

"You do realize that the only reason she's living is that I'm not a violent person," I said.

"Oh, I know! I kept trying to tell her--shut up Tammy--just shut up," Angela replied.

"Did she ever get it?" I asked.

"No. She never did. I tried to explain it to her. She said, oh, that's just Lisa. We always tease. She never did get it, but you know Tammy," Angela replied.

Angela and I got a chuckle as we told my vet what had happened. "Well, at least she provided us with some comic relief," he said. We laughed. We won.

I've told this story to several friends and when I tell Tammy's reply, "you just clean the sh** off the wall," you wouldn't believe how many of them jumped in the conversation and exclaimed, "DID YOU HIT HER?" No truer statement was ever spoken when I said I wasn't a violent person.

I see how people can kill in the heat of rage. My advice to the potential victim, "Back off. Better yet, be kind. What a person is going through in this life is sometimes unknown."

When all my senses and emotions were overextended, fortunately, I could still see Tammy's smiling face as a friend, clueless, but a well-meaning friend. Had she been a foe? God help her, because Angela wouldn't have had time.

Maybe it is not that you control your emotions, but you MUST control your actions.

4

Mava

I could look back and laugh at one of the worst days of my life because Mava was the one person to provide what I needed most.

She had been a friend of the family for decades, and my twelfth grade English teacher. She was one of those teachers you were afraid to get, but you knew you would; you were afraid to disappoint, and you tried never to do so. Mava was concise, disciplined, demanding, and kept you on your toes from the beginning of her class until the end. She could cut you down to size with a grimace, light you up with an approving smile and make your day with a wink. We all loved her.

She was at church every Sunday and she delivered the most hugs. She directed my wedding with just less than military "ten hut." No dilly dally, get in, get er done. And we did and had fun too.

Whenever I felt like venting, I would visit Mava. I was determined to flush all this unwelcomed anger, out of my system. One afternoon, my frustration climaxed with a boiling sensation from deep within. I don't remember the beginning of the conversation, but I vividly remember where it ended. Standing squarely in front of her, I forcefully unloaded the anger for losing my horse.

"... the F***ING THIS and the F***ING THAT, F***ING THIS and the F***ING THAT..."

While I was cursing with the utmost vigor, I was watching Mava standing stoic. She appeared completely undisturbed. I thought with all the effort I was putting into my speech, I would see her ears start to smoke and maybe sear off the sides of her head, but they never did. It was almost as if she were standing behind bulletproof glass. My ridiculous behavior didn't faze her in the least.

When I finished cursing a blue streak, I ended by saying, "I AM SORRY FOR MY LANGUAGE, AND I WILL BE SO HAPPY WHEN IT CLEARS UP!"

Mava, very quickly, concisely, almost with a rhythm said, "That's all right. Sometimes no other word describes it best."

She had tried her best to expand my vocabulary, when she had me in her class, and that day, the only word that I could think of was F***! As an "A" student, how stupid could I be? No one could have validated my feelings better that day than Mava, no matter how much I might pay a therapist. Priceless!

I have learned to appreciate four-letter words. Used wrong and they can be as harmful as bullets. Used right and they can be so perfect. Their use can open the vent on expressing anger. They give anger and frustration a place to go without hitting anyone or breaking anything: the common solution to anger management. And cheap, too.

5

The First Month

On Saturday, a sweet lady from the church called and asked if I could work in the kitchen for a potluck lunch at the church on Sunday. I had agreed a month earlier, and I was looking forward to it, as they rarely asked me to work in the kitchen. Currently, I knew I couldn't deal with all the smiling faces who would be there, and I didn't feel like being polite and happy. I just couldn't do it.

"Oh, sweetheart, have you heard my tale of woe?" I replied.

"Oh no, I haven't," she said in a very concerned tone.

"Well, I don't feel like telling it right now, but you can ask Mava, she knows. I'm so sorry. I was looking forward to helping out, but I can't do it right now." I said.

"Well, that's okay," she said in her sweet voice.

Only a great friend would volunteer to take care of my horses all week, and on Monday I went back to work. It took me three hours to clean three stalls when usually takes fifteen minutes. Some of the time I just sat, some of the time I had some phone calls, but slow motion was the best I could do.

The tractor bucket was full of the manure which I had cleaned out of the stalls. I drove the tractor down to the end of the barn and dismounted to open the barn doors.

I thought, "Now let me think about this a minute. Why am I so slow? The loss of my horse, which was my professional achievement, was like falling off the top rung of a ladder. If that fall had really happened, I would probably be in a body cast, and not moving at all, at least, I was mobile. Maybe this wasn't so bad after all."

I climbed back up on the tractor and decided maybe I was doing a little better than first thought. The shock was lingering.

By Wednesday, I finally got back to working horses. On Friday, I began feeling somewhat normal and I needed to focus on my other horses and get on with my program. I felt better about things until I made the mistake of going outside. I thought it was a good idea to put Mark's grave up on the hill where I could see it but found I couldn't bear to look in that direction. Whenever I walked to the car, I kept my eyes on the ground not to have to face the gravesite. If that wasn't bad enough, the sight of all the crummy fences I was going to replace with the money from the sale of Mark, just made me grit my teeth.

Another thing I was going to do with the money was to upgrade my tractor: equip it with a quick-change attachment to make the job of changing the bucket to the forklift easier. The first time I had to handle those greasy pins from changing the bucket to the forklift, I thought my head would explode. I didn't know which was greater, the anger or the frustration. It crossed my mind to kick the bucket, the tractor bucket that was, but I didn't want to add a broken toe to my misery. Who would have thought just going outside would stir up so much emotion? Little did I know just how many inner layers would reveal themselves in the months ahead.

Some people are born with the horse bug, and some people acquire it later in life. I was born with the bug. I wanted a horse for as long as I could remember. I was never so mad at my grandmother Worrell when she put trick candles on my birthday cake when I was about five or six. How could my secret birthday wish for a horse come true if I couldn't blow out the candles? What a cruel joke. She made all the family birthday cakes, and at that time I was furious at her sense of humor. At that age, I never even dreamed of a horse as great as the one I had just lost.

All my career I worked toward this dream and "poof" it was gone. I didn't even know if I still wanted to work with horses anymore. I had made some money along the way, but I certainly not any real money like what I would have made with Mark's sale. Even if I decided to quit, I had to keep working to disperse my hard-earned breeding stock and colts I had produced--years of work. But, this wasn't fun anymore. It once was wonderful to be able to enjoy my job and not just to be "working for the man" like so many Americans do. But all I could think about was now the time to quit?

Now, the two little word combination, "I quit," were becoming a bigger reality. I had never quit anything that I set out to do. I had achieved a lot with Mark. I had bred him, raised him, taught him to respect me, trained him, won three different divisions, collected semen to breed mares and produced frozen semen and raised his babies. The top accomplishment would have been to win a World's Championship and sell Mark for sizable money. He deserved a top honor. We almost made it to the top achievement.

It takes a lot of support to win at the top, and at the time I felt like I had none. My mom had recently remarried and quit coming to the barn, my friends had moved on to different barns, and my husband was complaining about money and me being away from home. There was no more Mark.

I wanted a press release to inform the public that I had hit one more rung on the career ladder; Mark was being sold to a known name family in the Saddlebred world, plus telling the horse world he was gone. After the initial shock, there was intense guilt and anger. It took almost a month after his death before I could think well enough to write. The press release touched on his winning accomplishments in a general way instead of listing them, because I thought thanking God for sending him to me in the first place was more important than first place ribbons.

He was a blessing in my life.

I never dreamed a press release could launch such a fiasco. As a courtesy, I requested permission from the agent to use the buyer's name in the press release. A few days passed, and he informed me the buyer didn't want to be attached to Mark's death, so the answer was no. I couldn't believe they would deny a simple request after all I had lost. I had bent over backwards extending the courtesy in letting them try him out at the agent's barn. A week's tryout turned into two months. The vet they selected for the pre-purchase exam was the one person involved in the deal who upset me the most. His involvement made a sweet deal go sour.

Fifteen years earlier, a fellow horseman warned me about this same vet. "You stay away from him. He will bad mouth all other vets, make you think he's God and do and charge whatever he wants." There are plenty of competent, ethical vets out there; I did as warned.

This was the verbal report I received after his exam:

"Well I have good news and bad news. The good news is your horse is sound. The bad news is he has an infection from the castration. Our vet said Mark needs twenty-one days of antibiotics; it probably won't fix it, he needs to go to a facility. Our vet said he can fix it, and you can pay for it," the agent said.

"Humph," I thought. "Who does he think he is prescribing for my horse? I didn't hire him. And since when does a vet dictate terms of a deal?"

I informed my vet of his findings. My vet said the medicine wouldn't fix the infection and to pick up my horse and he would fix it. The tug of war between treating my horse their way and my way began. But it was MY horse.

In time, just as the warning dictated, "he would bad mouth all other vets." It became evident their vet put the competency of my vet in question. I found it necessary to refuse a five-figure deposit in efforts to survive the pressure of pushing their vet on me. I could have used the money. In time, I made it clear to the agent, if they wanted their vet to treat my horse, they could pay for him and do as they please. My words didn't stop their pressure.

My vet graduated Magna Cum Laude from the Virginia/Maryland School of Veterinary Medicine. Questioning his competency was ridiculous, especially for such a simple surgery as castration. Any surgery can potentially have complications. I have used him very successfully for years and I trust his judgement.

It was intimidating to be up against a World Titles holding horse trainer, Dr. Supervet and the buyers/corporate America. Why did titles and big money give them power over what was mine? I had worked hard being able to train world-class horses and now I was swimming with the sharks. I gave into their vet's prescribed antibiotics because I was trying my best to keep all parties happy to complete the sale. His prescribed antibiotics not only didn't fix the problem, it added to Mark's demise. Two months of undue pressure took its toll on me, my vet, and Mark. Without the intrusion, odds were in our favor of successfully treating my horse.

Yet, all I asked for was permission to use their name in a press release. After they had pushed and pushed and pushed me to treat MY horse the way THEY wanted, I FINALLY pushed back.

The permission to use their name in the press release was granted.

I wrote an informative account describing the tragedy; all parties involved were devastated with the loss and gave an email for contact if anyone was so inclined. I sent it to the agent as a courtesy, on to the Saddlebred association, and waited for its release. To my chagrin, the association had taken liberties with MY WORK and changed the wording but put "as Whittle said." No one asked me for permission to change what I said yet put MY NAME on it. The line I was most irritated with was that I had set up an email "for Mark and me." They changed it to "for Mark." Now I ask you, who would email a dead horse?

The email address for a dead horse delivered all of five emails when thousands of people could access it. Was the wording the problem or are people just unable to reach out in a person's time of need? I had always been a very private person up to this point, and I wondered how I would handle putting the news out to the public. How would I feel when people brought up my loss? It surprised me.

My loss felt as though a ton of bricks had fallen on me. Mark's death was crushing. Every time someone called, a brick was lifted. Some people were skilled enough to lift many bricks. I found myself wanting more friends to help lighten my load. It didn't even matter what they said, just acknowledged my pain.

Before this tragedy, I was unable to reach out, because I didn't know what to say. I now make an effort to acknowledge people's pain and even saying "I'm so sorry, I don't know what to say" lifts bricks. Even a caring look or a touch on the arm with no words spoken takes off a brick. A card is nice.

The five people who took the time to answer an email, I can't tell you how much I thank you. One man from Canada didn't email, he took the time to call and share the loss of his stallion the winter before. I was grateful. Another email was from an unfamiliar horse lady who shared her sympathy. Her skill lifted several bricks. Three were friends, and one was with me in the horse program at MSU. He was my assistant selling pictures when I was the official equine photographer at a Kentucky horse show. The sky was so black in one direction we couldn't see where the sky and ground met. The show was called off and we ran from the approaching storm. We had survived the horrifying experience. Laughing and catching up with this old friend lifted more than bricks. It lifted my spirit.

I shared my horror story about the buyer's vet, and the number of stories that came out of the woodwork from other people about the same vet was astounding. I tried to get these people, along with me, to report him his unethical behavior to the State Board of Veterinary

Examiners, but no one was willing to be brave. I didn't think my one report would amount to anything significant, so for the time being, I gave up on doing the right thing.

6

The Next Four Months

It was April, and the weather was beginning to turn warm. I had waited since last spring to have my 1961 English style Massey Ferguson 35 tractor painted. My farm help who fed my horses for years had been bragging all winter that he was a great body man, and he could do an excellent job for me. Days of seventy-degree weather, and I kept telling him I wanted it ready to mow hay in May, and the time was right to paint the tractor. His excuse not to do it that day was because he needed to wait for the metal to warm up. How stupid did he think I was? At seventy degrees in sunlight, the metal was warm. Metal was not like the ground which took several weeks to warm up before planting. If there was any excuse, he could find it.

That night, I let YouTube educate me on the finer points of bodywork. The next day, I began working on the tractor bodywork myself. I had no idea how therapeutic Bondo could be. Bondo was used to fill in the dents for a smooth body finish before painting. Its consistency was like pottery clay but smoother. Smear on Bondo with a wide hand-held spatula and smooth it like peanut butter. Let dry and sand. Perfect, somewhat mindless work for a grief-stricken brain like mine. I looked forward to it every day after working horses--a productive therapeutic exercise.

After days and days, maybe weeks, the bodywork was complete. My farm help showed up, painted the tractor, and tried to take all the credit. It looked like it had just been driven off the showroom floor more than 50 years ago. The winter before, we had replaced and rebuilt many mechanical parts. A masterpiece, if I say so myself.

May rolled around, and the hay was ready to cut at the same time as the Asheville Horse Show. I had planned to get away and meet friends there, but I needed to make sure all equipment was working before I left my farm help to mow and tedder. We hooked up my new drum mower to my beautiful refurbished tractor, and I was so happy the new combination could handle my thick stand of grass. I made half a lap around the hayfield with a perfect cut, and then the tractor engine blew up. Pulling the hill, plus the dense stand of grass, along with the drum mower, was a load more than the engine could handle. It didn't entirely give up because it could at least limp to the barn. So much for the horse show, not to mention my beautiful tractor. More anger seethed out. Would there be any end to my misery?

A high school boyfriend had offered his tractor if I ever needed one, so I texted him, "Hay down, need tractor." I didn't know if I would hear from him the way my luck had been running. I was relieved when he responded quickly and said he would have his tractor there the next morning. I knew my farm help would be jealous because he kept offering his old tractor. I had tried his way the year before, and I was so sick of him and his tractor by the end of the job, I wasn't going through that again. My high school friend was going to deliver his tractor when my farm help wasn't there. I met him at the barn, and we caught each other up on our other high school friends. Old friends who went through all twelve school grades with you can sure lift a soul's spirit. He and his tractor saved the day.

All went well until my farm help showed up and it was obvious to me he was mad. My friend didn't catch on to my help's male territorial dance. I thought at any minute he was going to pee on the tractor tire to mark his territory. He managed to run my friend off, and I had been enjoying the visit. I was already irritated with my farm help because I had to fix the one piece of hay equipment he was supposed to have ready, the tedder. If that weren't irritating enough, he wouldn't leave. I didn't need his help. I needed him to have already completed the job.

He is strong as an ox, and with his bare hands, he bends the tedder arms which are a quarter inch thick. I have to heat the arms in the forge, beat it with a hammer to bend them. My way is a little more accurate. I attach the adjusted tedder arm, but it rocks on the mount.

"Well, you bent it wrong," my farm help announced.

I took the tedder arm off and sighted for straightness, and it couldn't have been better. The place of attachment was bent and needed hitting from bottom up. I took a four-pound sledgehammer to hit from the bottom. One hit and I knew I couldn't bend the metal. I wasn't sure anybody could.

My help was grumbling, and I showed him the problem.

"Well, you hit it wrong," he said.

I had had enough and dropped my tools to the ground and arms to my sides and said, "Well, apparently I can't do anything right. I..."

Before I could get the next sentence out, he interrupts.

"Well, if you are gonna have a pity party, I'm out of here. Do you want your keys?" he asked.

"What keys?" I replied.

"The keys to the gate and office," he said.

He has quit on me countless times over the last ten years, but he has never offered up his keys. My hand shot out like a switchblade knife to accept those keys and rid myself of his sorry ass.

Instantly, it was my job to do all the feeding, stall cleaning, working horses, plus mowing, teddering and baling 390 bales of hay. The death of my horse might kill me, but I wasn't going to let my farm help do me in. Best conditioned, quality hay I had ever put up.

My son and his friend, both fourteen, and two Mennonite boys, picked up and stacked the hay bales. I told my son and his friend to keep up with the other two, who knew how to work. One was grabbing a bale in each hand, pitching the hay on the trailer and running to the next bale while the other was stacking. My son and his friend couldn't quite keep up, but they were trying, and all were having fun working.

I was doubly pleased when I paid them, and they looked at each other, smiled and asked, "Can we go to the movies?!"

"It is your money, you've worked for it, and if that's what you want to do, it's okay with me!" I said with a smile.

They were so tickled with themselves. I delighted in teaching the boys the value of a day's work and to see them enjoy the money they had earned.

June rolled around, and I had planned to take horses to the Blowing Rock Horse Show where I had many fun times, and great memories with Mark and friends. Two months earlier, I had managed to take two horses to the Bonnie Blue Show in Lexington, Virginia, for practice and not to show. It was not one of my regular shows with Mark, so I didn't have to face memories. I was trying my best to move on from my grief, but I realized when asked what happened to Mark, it was almost more than I could do to hold in my anger. I was barely ready to be in public.

Now I was planning to go to Blowing Rock. I had a lot of great memories and wins with Mark at that show. He had won the Park class one year and the Five-Gaited Grand Championship the next. I had planned to go a day early and take a horse to show. The night before, I couldn't pack my clothes without a meltdown. I decided to go a day later. The next day, the show manager called to see if I was coming and I said, "Tomorrow." That night, I finally finished the packing my clothes, after another meltdown or two.

The next day when I got to the barn, I never even attempted to pack all the stuff required to show a horse. Another meltdown and I finally gave up that I couldn't do it. The management called to ask if I was coming, and I said I was unable to bring a horse, but I would be there tomorrow to pay my bill. I still planned on going, at least, to meet a friend.

I had been thinking of sending my two working horses to Kentucky for sale, and after this impossible feat of not being able to get my sh** together to get the horse to the show, I decided now was the time. I drove to Blowing Rock and felt shell-shocked when I walked onto the grounds. I still couldn't believe a horse could affect me so much. I went in to pay for the stalls I had reserved and the only words I could get out of my mouth was, "I lost Mark."

I felt a little better when I met up with my friend, and some people said they had been thinking about me. A few more bricks seemed to be lifted off. Their kind words picked me up, and I was grateful. Other friends just looked my way but didn't say a thing. I guess they didn't know what to say. I ran into one friend, George, who had followed Mark's and my career. He had enjoyed watching us show at Roanoke. He said it was such a delight to see the two of us together. I had even won the Perpetual Trophy he donated to the show. I told him just how depressed I had been and how I had decided it would be a loud and open recovery. I was sending my other show horses to Kentucky for sale, and I just needed a break. My family had planned a trip out west next month.

"That's a good idea. You know that's what I do. I'm a grief counselor at the church in Roanoke," he said.

"Can you help me out?" I asked.

"You're doing the right thing, and I completely understand how you feel," he said with a polite chuckle. I felt guilty for losing Mark and for not simply being able to move on from a loss of just a horse. His encouragement and understanding removed many bricks.

He shared one of his personal traumas. It helped me realize I wasn't the only one who struggled with grief. He removed another brick.

I was glad I ran into him.

The trip out west was a month away. It was the same amount of time before the stalls would be open at the stable where I was planning to send my horses. As much as I wanted a break, it seemed like relief would never come. As hard as I tried working my other show horses, my heart just wasn't in it. They just reminded me of the loss of Mark and how close I had come to reaching a lifelong dream. I needed more time to heal.

The horses left for Kentucky the day after I left for California. I wanted a break from working horses and going to the barn. Still, four months into this grieving process, every night of my sleep had been disturbed rolling over and over in my mind, "What did I do wrong?"

A couple of weeks before the trip, one of Mom's friends and her daughter, came to visit her. I had known them since I was a child. They wanted to see me. I hated to go anywhere I didn't have to as my little black cloud went everywhere I did. It was nice to see them, but I didn't pretend to be happy. After a short time, I excused myself to leave, and my friend followed me outside.

"You know, I feel like I just lost everything, my horse, my success, not to mention the money," I said.

"But you still have your success," she said very kindly with a great smile.

It took awhile to soak in. I DID still have my success! All along, I felt like without Mark; I couldn't prove myself. But I had ALREADY proved myself. What a wonderful revelation! And I so appreciated my friend pointing it out. Her words were sweet.

"No one can ever take away what you know," were the words shared with me years ago from one of the greatest horsewomen in the Saddlebred world. At the time, I wondered what on earth had happened to her to give me such advice. I didn't think I would ever need it, but I did store it away. Now I understand the wisdom in her words.

More clarity crept in. All along, I felt like everyone was thinking, "Why doesn't Lisa get on with it, she's got more colts." Looking back, I don't think anyone was thinking that and most people just had their own problems, not to be dwelling on mine. Who is "everybody" anyway?

It was a good day when I realized, "Yes, I can do it again. I can develop another nice horse and I was just as good as anyone else. We all have ups and downs, failures and successes."

It would have been easier for me to work horses with two broken legs than a broken heart. I just didn't **want** to work, ride, or even see another horse. To keep up with my responsibilities I had to work. The horses added to my heavy heart. At least I was a little stronger than my tractor. It blew the pistons in the engine while pulling the hill with the mower in tow. I guess I was lucky enough to pull my load, but nowhere near full power. Now I understood how stress could cause heart attacks. Luckily, I fared better than my tractor.

I worked and worked to lighten my load and my trip was upon us. My horses were going to Kentucky and my family and I were going to explore the West. My journey had brought me to the bottom of my pit of despair, and I was about to begin the climb up the other side.

With a little better attitude, I went to church for the first time since I had lost Mark. On the way out, I was greeted by the preacher where he stood by the doorway every Sunday. He asked if I would I meet with him in his office, because he had something to talk about with me. I knew it was about the church's website we were developing. I told him I was going out west for ten days and I would be glad to speak with him when I returned.

Now, thank God, I would have a break from horses.

III

Sheer Delight

7

Our Trip Out West

Our trip out west was a chance to visit Tom's daughter, husband, and their two children. It had been several years since we had been to California. I liked his daughter and her family.

Late spring, Tom suggested visiting and turned to me.

"I bet you won't take off enough time," he said.

I said pretty quickly, "Try me. I'm ready to take off three months and drive across America."

In the past, horse shows had kept me from taking any extended time off. I would either be at a show or preparing for one. I wasn't the least bit interested in showing a horse. I was thinking about quitting anyway.

We began to think about the trip and plan. Train trips looked like a fun way to get all the way across America, instead of driving. We decided to fly to Los Angeles, stay one night with his daughter's family, pile into their Toyota van, drive to Williams, Arizona and catch a ride on the Grand Canyon Railway. Our adventure began.

On the drive to the railway was the only time his daughter and I spoke of my loss. I was still trying to figure out why such a great horse died under my watch. Damned if the black cloud of sorrow hadn't followed me all the way to California. I wasn't the least bit surprised because, no matter where I ran, I couldn't get away from myself. We didn't talk about it anymore, but a lot of the time, my black cloud was evident on my face. I still wasn't sleeping very well.

We traveled for several hours to our destination town of Williams. The landscape on the western side of America was so different from the landscape on the eastern side. All I needed for entertainment was to look out the window. We arrived in Williams around 5 pm in time to check into our rooms, explore the little town and have dinner. The kids had fun on a ski lift that went high enough to see the entire village. The next morning before boarding, the train company put on a fun western skit against the backdrop of a western town complete with horses, cowboys, a sheriff and a shootout. The good guys won.

We boarded the train and started the expedition to the Grand Canyon. The train trolled along to make it easy to take in the landscape, not like the speed of Amtrak. Most of the land was flat with scruffy vegetation and often, not a tree to be found. There were usually mountains far off in the distance which jutted straight up out of the flatness and was flat on top. If they had some shape to them, they had names like Sleeping Indian Mountain. It did look like a person sleeping.

I started looking for water. We saw not a stream, nor a river, nor a pond, nor a lake. Several times, I saw what I thought was a creek bed, and a culvert under a road, but no water. I pointed this out, and everybody started looking for water. There was a bar in the adjacent railcar complete with ice cream and refreshments, so it wasn't like we were about to die of thirst. The funny thing was when a small watering hole appeared, we all took a picture of it. I learned in certain seasons, all those creek beds are full and flash floods can sometimes fill them in an instant. Most places, it looked like there hadn't been water for years, not just weeks or months. It was very different from the lush greenery of Virginia.

There were some industrial sites, homes, and cattle, but vastness like what I saw in the westerns when I was growing up. Trees started to show up when we got closer to the Grand Canyon with more roll to the landscape. The train pulled to a stop, and everyone got off to explore the south rim of the canyon.

The view and size of the Grand Canyon are magnificent. The Canyon's colors are beautiful and change throughout the day with the help of the sun and clouds overhead. I'm sure the moon and seasons are additional brushes to add their flavor of color, in addition to the spice the weather can add. What God can paint when he wants is spectacular beyond belief. I can only imagine all the variations of sunrise and sunset.

We explored various trails, but to go down the Canyon wall where the mules carry their passengers and packs, whew. It takes a brave soul to undertake the journey, and countless people do it every year. A wall on one side that goes straight up and the wall on the other that goes straight down. Only one pack mule has ever been lost. I see what "sure-footed as a mule" really means.

It was a beautiful day at the Grand Canyon National Park. Late in the afternoon, we boarded the same train for the ride home. On the way to the Canyon, we were entertained on the train by some singing cowboys. On the way back, the train attendant told us there would be a mock train robbery, not to be alarmed.

I thought, "Why would he give away the element of surprise?"

In his next breath, he said, "And if you are wondering why I'm telling you this and taking away the surprise, it is because last year when the cowboy appeared on the train with a gun, a foreigner, who didn't speak English, thought it was a terrorist act and pinned the poor cowboy actor to the ground. So, we are letting you know it is just for fun."

I wished the foreigner could have been around in the right place during 911. Maybe he had never seen an American western or perhaps he just commonly lived under more fear than we Americans did. I still had to respect the foreigner for his mistake. We chuckled at the thought. The cowboys rode up on horses, fired shots, boarded the train and robbed people of tips or whatever we were freely willing to give. It was a fun and somewhat a relief that the perceived horror of being at gunpoint was not real; just a taste of the old west and a tinge of our new world.

We left Williams the next morning after breakfast at the Pine Country Restaurant. I bought a souvenir coffee cup from the place with its name on one side and Historic Highway 66 emblem on the other. Highway 66 was the first major US designated highway, and it spanned 2400 miles from Chicago, Illinois, to Santa Monica, California, passing through six other states on the way. It inspired the song "Get your Kicks on Route 66." John Steinbeck's "The Grapes of Wrath" used Route 66 in the movie which mimicked what happened in 1930 during The Dust Bowl era when farm families had to leave and travel to California for work. Disney's' "Cars" depicted how once thriving towns died after interstates took traffic away. Somewhere along our travel, we took a family picture standing on the highway with the painted Highway 66 emblem at our feet. A keychain of the old road was collected as an ornament for my Christmas tree. I liked rather inexpensive souvenirs like coffee cups and Christmas ornaments to remind me of the fun of past experiences. This trip was a gold mine for our Christmas tree.

Our final destination for the day was Sedona, Arizona, where we went by way of Jerome, Arizona, a tourist spot known as a ghost town. It was a side trip on a side road that at times was as scary as the mule trail along the Grand Canyon. It had many hairpins turns to wind up the mountain and then wind down. Hairpin curves are in Virginia. In Arizona, they are called switchbacks.

Jerome, Arizona, thrived in early 1900 with up to 15,000 people, as it was home to the largest copper mine in the world. All the copper had been mined out, and the town had dried up to less than five hundred folks. The citizens were keeping it alive and anyone you met made sure you were having a good time. A friendly flavor not just anywhere can recreate. There was a graveyard of cars and trucks that dated back to almost the beginning of cars and displayed an electric Studebaker in excellent condition. I never even knew they made such a thing so long ago. We had a grand view overlooking the Arizona landscape through a giant picture window while eating at the Haunted Hamburger. Who could pass up a place named like that?

After lunch, we continued our journey to Sedona for a few days stop. I've been to quaint small towns that have sign ordinances, make themselves so inviting you want to stay, but Sedona must have had building ordinances. The houses and building went so harmoniously with the landscape; they looked more like they had grown there. The red rocks of Sedona uniquely color the view and many houses would be red terra cotta or light tans like some of the other mountains, or even olive green like some of the greenery. Its unique beauty was very different from the South where I live.

One day, we took a guided hike and explored a cliff dwelling. They were the homes to the native Americans hundreds of years ago. One was later inhabited by a settler who was using a small water source to irrigate his farming project. He decided to dynamite the water source to make it bigger and unfortunately, split the earth, which made the water run underground. He lost the entire water source and ruined his productive farming. I had seen an old western movie the night before, in which a "greenhorn," as John Wayne put it, had dynamited the waterhole that was the only water source before crossing the desert. Reality had to be the inspiration for the movie. The area in Arizona, Utah, and Nevada was the backdrop for many westerns. It was fun to see in real life. A local movie museum showed how they made westerns and the economic impact on the area.

The next stop was Antelope Canyon near Page, Arizona. It was a slot canyon on Navajo land, and the Navajos guided the tours. The day we were there it was ninety-six degrees, and we were driven to the canyon in the back of a truck with benches and guard rails for safety.

They hauled us out of town on the road and then off the road and in what looked like a dry riverbed, flying at speeds higher than fifty miles an hour on the flat, sandy desert-like terrain. The ninety-six-degree dry temperature was still ninety-six degrees at fifty miles an hour. I never experienced moving air not being somewhat cooling until then. It was just plain hot.

Flash floods eroded the Navajo sandstone to form Antelope Canyon. The swirling water and sand running through the canyon created the most beautiful flowing patterns on the walls. The section I liked the best displayed the look of a horse. The entire exploration was on flat ground with no climbing. It was most interesting to see and experience. Our Navajo guide spoke several different languages, accommodating people from around the world.

We left Page, Arizona, and continued our journey into Utah with our next destination, Zion National Park. The landscape started to change color from less of the red mountains to a beige sandstone with red stripes. The flat land took on more vegetation and crops. I was thrilled to see a most beautiful stand of protein-rich alfalfa which also grows on the eastern side of the US. We paid a fee to enter the National Park, and as we went around a sweeping curve, the mountains rose up around us. In seconds, the terrain was unbelievable, with rugged, slanted rock of white and red color. A desert bighorn sheep graced our path and deer to boot. In the heart of the Park, there was a spectacular mountain view complete with a colorful rainbow. We could have spent a week exploring, but a drive through was all we had planned. I wouldn't have missed it for the world. We spent the night in St. George, Utah, and Tom met up with a cousin he hadn't seen since they were kids.

The next day, we headed to Nevada to its oldest State Park called the Valley of Fire. It was formed from Aztec sandstone 150 million years ago during the time of dinosaurs. The sandstone appeared to be on fire as it reflected the sun's rays. We could have spent all day, but we drove through the park and took a couple of short hikes. We drove on to Lake Mead and had lunch at the marina. On the way out, I bought a bag of popcorn to feed the fish. As we started feeding the fish off the dock, hundreds came up to wait for the popcorn. An ocean of dark fish with pink mouths opened to catch the popcorn. Fish layered and layered on top of more fish. One of the strangest sights I had ever seen.

Off we went to Hoover Dam. The landscape in Nevada was entirely like nothing I had ever seen before. I was glad I didn't doze off because if I had, when I awoke, I would have thought I had just landed on the surface of the moon. No vegetation whatsoever. It was unbelievably ugly; maybe someone could call the view pretty, maybe not. I had no idea we could spend an entire day at Hoover Dam. What a man-made wonder across the Colorado River, with one side in Nevada and the other in Arizona. I captured a beautiful artistic picture of the bridge overhead. It was amazing what man can accomplish. It was a manufacturing feat second to none. The dam supplied electricity to Arizona, Nevada, and parts of California.

We finished our day driving into the man-made wonder of Las Vegas. The sunset was spectacular. Parking was free, but a hotdog was nine dollars. At the high school football games at home, hotdogs are two dollars, and they support the team. I guess a nine-dollar hotdog supports Las Vegas. A driving tour of the famous strip included a look of Egypt, Italy, New York, France and almost anything else the imagination could dream. Since our youngest traveler was five, we skipped the casinos. I wasn't interested in trying my luck because I had spent the last five months trying to survive my bad luck. I wasn't ready to test it.

The next day, we took in the Gold and Silver Pawn Shop made famous by Pawn Stars. Tom's son-in-law couldn't turn down the rock group KISS putt putt--wholesome family fun in the midst of sin city.

It was time to go back to California. I didn't like the thought of going home. I just wanted to keep going and going. This experience was way more delightful than what I had left back home. Our journey took us through the Mojave Desert. I don't think we could have experienced the real heat more than when our van's air conditioning crashed when the outside temperature was one hundred thirteen degrees. Six people in a van from ages five to seventy-three. Hot, blowing air doesn't cool, it just whips hair around. The best cooling idea was two bags of ice in a cooler for us to crunch and smear on our skin. The ice worked to keep us from overheating. My son popped up with reading riddles off his phone to entertain us to forget the misery. His idea worked like a charm. Thinking, laughing and ice cubes solved our would-be desert disaster.

We arrived safe and sound and had one more day before flying home. We decided to explore the California Science Center which was the highlight of my husband's trip. He got to see the Space Shuttle Endeavor. He was like a kid in the candy shop when he saw the Endeavor for the first time. It was vast, and he read every display. We all enjoyed it.

The night before we left, Tom's daughter and I finally sat down to talk. She has a Masters in Family Counseling, and I had been looking forward to talking with her. I told her how tired I was of my grief and asked when would it go away.

"I hear you want the pain to go away," she said.

"How do I get rid of it?" I asked.

"It's different for different people," she said.

"Well, I'm ready to get rid of it," I said.

I will say that getting away for a change of scenery did me a lot of good. Seeing God's pits such as the Grand Canyon and Antelope Canyon were way better than seeing my pit of despair. It gave me a break from my broken record of trying to figure out what I had done wrong. As we talked, I said I made the mistake of giving up control of my work, and I will never do that again.

I had learned early in my life, that people who don't make mistakes are people who don't DO anything. I am okay with making mistakes, but I hate to make the same mistake twice. I want to make a new one. She laughed at the comment. I also told her I knew no matter where you run; you can't get away from yourself. I knew early on to plunge into my grief to eventually get through it. She liked that one too. Our conversation ended with a lighter heart.

We flew home and rested up after our marathon trip.

I was at the barn. I finally realized: even if I had done something different, it may not have changed the outcome. I had forgiven myself. Then I asked God to forgive me too. I will never forget the feeling forgiveness brought. Peace came over me like a warm, anointing oil flowing over my entire body. A peace I never knew existed. I guess it was that "come to Jesus" moment I've always heard described. It was the most wonderful feeling I have ever had.

Forgiveness had the greatest power.

8

Fond Memories

What an incredible feeling peace was for me. I was so happy. I didn't have any horses to work, and it was about ten days before my son's school started, and for the first time I was entirely off from work. Nothing pressing, no horses to work and I could do whatever I wanted. My son and I went to the barn and had so much fun being silly. He begged me to quit making him laugh.

"Why are we laughing so much!" he said.

"Why, don't you like it?" I replied.

"I'm just not used to it," he said a little puzzled.

We had a ball during the last days of summer vacation. I was just so happy to be free from grief, free from working horses at last and most of all, I was having fun with my son.

Some of the fun memories with Mark began to come back. I thought of the time I showed at the North Carolina Championship in pretty deep competition. Sometimes in competition, I try too hard to make a good show, but I don't let loose and go for the win. The qualifying class was one of those rides where Mark had more to give, but I didn't ask him to give it. My friend, Peyton, was the paddock master and he became the self-appointed cheering squad and support group I needed. The next couple of days he kept pumping me up for the Friday night ride. My biggest competition was a veteran of the show ring with a beautiful bay gelding with a big knee popping trot. Peyton kept after me to smoke her at the rack and convinced me I had the horse to do it. It took him two days to talk me into laying it on the line and pick the veteran off at the rack. By the time the day came, and the class was up, I was ready to go for it! It was the last class of the evening and Peyton was off duty and he showed up to coach. I finished the first way thinking I did pretty good, I looked over at Peyton.

"You gotta do better than that," he said.

That was it! This was going to be "the rip your clothes off on the beach" kind of ride! I'm gonna lay it all on the line! The class reversed, and the ride was on! Mark's rack that night was one of the greatest rides I ever had! First, was the slow gait and I couldn't find my biggest competition anywhere. "Rack on," called the announcer and I squeezed Mark into rack and kept asking him for more and more and he kept giving and giving! It was a fantastic ride on my beautiful stallion! The wind whipped past my ears like riding my bicycle downhill when I was a kid! Whirwhirwhirwhirwhirwhirwhir, was the sound of the wind whipping past my ears! It was a feeling next to flying! Flying on a winged Pegasus! His rack was so smooth, it was like his feet never touched the ground! Whir Whir Whir Whir Whir Whir Whir! My competition ended up winning the class, but with a ride like that, who cares! It wasn't the color of the ribbon that was worth remembering, it was all about the ride!

I glanced over at Peyton as I rode by and he said, "Now that's more like it!"

I laughed out loud as I rode past my friend!

"Peyton, I couldn't find my competition," I said after the class.

"That's okay, she was watching out for you," he chuckled.

We both got a great laugh and joy out of the whole experience! Even better, how many people told me how much they enjoyed watching my ride with Mark, and how they would have judged it differently. What a fun memory!

But the fun didn't end with the ride. I was stabled apart from my friends, Shelley and Beverly this time. I took Mark to my stabling, cooled him, and carefully put him up for the night. I rode my scooter to their barn, and when I rounded the corner, Shelley jumped up out of her chair, pulled Beverly out of her seat in the middle of the barn aisle. With their hands in the air, they began bowing and bowing, up and down, up and down. It was praise for the queen! We burst into laughter!

"This is great! But that's not what I expected from you two. I thought you were gonna say I needed to sit up straighter or something!" I laughed.

"Oh no, that was awesome! "they exclaimed.

Oh my gosh, we laughed until we almost cried! That was one of the greatest rides I ever had! How lucky could I be to have the ride to look back on and friends to share it.

9

Shelley and Beverly

The pleasant memory of Mark and my horse show girlfriends led me back to thinking about how our friendship began. It all started one year at Blowing Rock Horse Show when I was working with a North Carolina stable during the show. The trainer and I were friends, and we had a simple agreement. I would help him with his horses, and he would help me with mine. His horses were customers' horses, and mine was my own. No money exchanged hands, you help me, and I help you. It worked.

My husband, son and I were RV camping at the show, and I enjoyed getting up early, feeding horses and cleaning stalls before breakfast. There was no better breakfast than home cooked eggs, bacon, toast, fruit, juice, and coffee or whatever you could pile on when camping. No restaurant could compare. Add a little work before, and breakfast never tasted so good!

I was having a good time and when work was fun, outside, with beautiful horses, friends, family and sporty competition, what could be better! My son joined in on the chores and he became thrilled to find out Shelley and Beverly would tip him to help care for their horses. He was trying to earn enough money to buy an Xbox. Yet another opportunity to teach my son a lesson on making his own money was priceless. Life was good!

One afternoon, Shelley and Beverly had decided to wash the tail on one of the Saddlebreds Shelley had brought to Blowing Rock to trail ride during the weekend. The trails could be easily accessed from the show grounds, and the scenery took in beautiful mountain views and woodsy trails. Her trail horses were stabled alongside the show horses. She asked me to help with the tail washing task. Off we went to the wash area where Shelley tied the horse to the fence leaving all three of us to wash the tail. I stood there holding and dispensing shampoo while watching the other two, up to their elbows in water and shampoo, washing the horse's tail to their heart's content. They looked like two little girls playing with a Barbie doll. Horses had a way of bringing out the kid in anyone. I was watching the contentment found in this small task and knew they were having fun, and I decided to add to the fun by making a joke. One person was enough to accomplish this task of tail washing, but there were three of us with our hands in shampoo.

Thinking I was so smart, I popped up and said, "How many Pollocks does it take to wash a horse's tail?" Beverly started giggling, and Shelley's eyes popped out and said, in a high-pitched dynamic way, "LLLIISSSAAA... BEVERLY IS POLISH!" My eyes popped out, my mouth flew open, and apologies began to fly. When I saw tears of laughter streaming down Beverly's face, I knew it wasn't the end, but the beginning of a beautiful friendship. With the amount of laughter my stupidity produced, I could say it was a great joke, but the punchline backfired, and the joke was on me. It was well deserved and nothing I had expected.

The two ladies were always referred to by the men at the stables as "The Blondes." The connotation hinted "dumb", but it was never said, nor did it fit. I was not a member of this group because I was not blonde, and we were all far from dumb. But shortly after my joke, I quickly realized there was nothing STUPIDER than a SMART brunette! From that blunder moment on, I was no longer an outsider and our little horse show group began. For the next few years, our fun was priceless.

The same year Mark and I, with the trainer's help, won the Open Park Championship. The following year, I gave the trainer the ride in the Five-Gaited Grand Championship. He put in a good solid ride and won with ease, a good lesson for me from a seasoned veteran.

There were several things I remember about his ride, but what I remember most about this win was the presentation photo. Most of the time I prefer the victory pass photo, but in the sloppy conditions of the ring due to rain, before the trainer could make the coveted victory pass, one of Mark's front shoes was sucked off by the sloppy ground. On the first glance, the photo was a crummy picture in content. I had joined him in the winner's circle with mud all over my shoes and all over the underside, feet and legs of Mark. I put one arm around the trainer and with a sleeveless blouse, my armpit showed in the picture, Mark had his shoe missing, and the trainer was about to burst out of his suit. But to look a little closer, the beauty in the picture was two friends supporting each other. I gave my friend a solid contender after he had lost some longtime customers, while he gave me the top placing and prize money to pay for my expenses. Truly a wonderful picture!

10

Prior Work Experiences

I thought back to my work experience in Kentucky more than twenty-five years ago, when I was working horses for a man in his sixties. He had gained his expertise under the direction of well-known brothers, who had many World Champions to their credit. I took the job to supplement my income while I was working as a freelance artist. Working horses was different from my prior office job as a graphic artist/assistant art director. I thought working outside would be a pleasant relief from the high paced pressure of the thoroughbred horse advertising world.

When I realized the skill and development in training horses was a viable industry, I became hooked. I thought I was fortunate to work under a skilled horseman and only the two of us were responsible for developing his stock. I didn't have to compete with who rode what horse. I knew he had the reputation of being a dirty old man, but I thought I was capable of handling his advances, and I was, but his demeaning words eventually took their toll. I was careful about what places I went with him in public.

We had a love/hate relationship. Some days, I loved working horses with him, and other days, I hated the ground he walked on. I remembered one Sunday morning, he called early and woke me up. It was my only day off, and I loved my sleep.

I answered the phone, "Hello?"

"How about I come up there and have a cup of coffee?" he said.

"No," I replied.

"Oh yeah. I'll be right there, come in, and we'll have a cup of coffee," my boss said.

"NO!" I replied.

"It's a beautiful day. I'll be right there," he persisted.

"I SAID NO. You're not coming up here, and furthermore, you woke me up on my only day off!" I slammed the phone down.

He never showed up, and I never went back to sleep.

The next morning, I walked into work as usual, and there was a liver chestnut stud pony tied in the barn aisle way. My boss was sitting close by, and I said, "Mornin'," as I walked by his chair.

"You know. You'll never make it in this business. I called you to come and go with me to pick up this pony, and it was an opportunity for you to make a new contact in this business. You'll never make it in this business," he said.

I stopped dead in my tracks, turned around, marched up to his chair and pointed my finger in his face. "You didn't ASK me to go get a pony. You asked to come for coffee and STICK your foot in my door. Had you asked me to get the pony, I would have gone. So you can stop this game right now!" I would **rot** before I gave in.

If looks could kill, we both were dead. I went on to my job while my boss cooked up my punishment for not getting his way. After cleaning stalls each morning, we had gotten in the habit of driving to a nearby country store, and he would buy me an eighty-nine-cent honey bun. It was a nice break before working with horses. I didn't need to eat twice, so I stopped eating before work. On this day, when it came time for my breakfast, he was demanding I ride the first horse. Where was my honey bun?

When I stepped off the first horse, and onto the ground, my sugar dropped to the floor. I was not diabetic, but my body was used to the massive amount of sugar from the honey bun, and it wasn't there. My arms and legs felt like lead, and my mind and vision were fuzzy. I couldn't drive to get the bun myself. It was a miracle that only my sugar hit the ground.

"Hey, I need that honey bun because my sugar has dropped," I begged.

"H*ll no!" he scolded.

I could barely function. My body eventually compensated. I finally made it to lunch and through the rest of the day. I swore I would never let anyone be responsible for my breakfast again. In a few days, after he got past being angry at my refusal, he asked me to ride with him to the store. Did he think I would let him set me up like that again?

"H*ll no," was my reply and I ended the joy riding for breakfast. A**hole.

On another note, the biggest lesson I walked away with happened one day when I stopped another advance, and he gave me a great cussing. I usually ignored it, but finally, I gave him a cussing back. I felt terrible all day after the exchange. It wasn't what he had said to me that hurt; it was the words I had chosen to say to him. I decided that day, "Just because you are an A**HOLE, doesn't mean I have to be." So, when he cussed me, I just smiled. I won.

I held my own when needed and continued to learn lots of good, and some bad lessons. Most of the time, we had a world of fun. Many things he said stuck with me even today, and in some instances, the longer he was dead, the smarter he got. At this time of Mark's loss, I could hear him so plainly say, "Horses. They will build you up, just to break your heart."

I hate that he was right.

This reminded me, not of his heartbreaks, but his heart attacks...one potential and one real.

On a ninety-six-degree, humid day, my boss decided to bed stalls. He used a tractor with a front-end loader to put one load of sawdust bedding in front of each stall door. Usually, we both shoveled the bedding into the stalls, but my boss conveniently disappeared. I shoveled and shoveled. Sweat was rolling off my brow and into my eyes. The saltiness burned. Not only did my eyebrows quit working, apparently, my boss did too. I went to look for him, and to my disgust, he was laid out in his recliner asleep! He was twitching his nose and swatting around his face. Was he asleep or was he messing with me? I went back to shoveling. I completed pitching the sawdust into a stall and went back to check if he was awake. Same thing. Animation and all. I shoveled, sweated, checked...shoveled, sweated, checked.

I was convinced my boss was messing with me, rubbing it in I was doing all the work when it was hotter than h*ll, and he was leisurely taking a nap. I picked up a five-gallon bucket with about one inch of water in it. I stood at the door swirling the water in the bucket while he twitched his nose and swatted around his face. Finally, I had had enough and decided to teach him a lesson. I tossed a narrow stream of water above him, not to hit him in the face. The little stream stopped in mid-air and dropped all at once. The second it fell, he rose directly out of his chair, righted himself in mid-air, and landed on his feet. My fun turned to horror as I saw his eyes rolling around and around while his head twitched rhythmically to the left. His words came out in a stutter, "Li....Li....Li....Li... LLLIIISSSAAA!" My heart hit the floor as I thought "OH, SH**! I'VE JUST GIVEN HIM A HEART ATTACK! HOW COULD I BE SO STUPID?!"

When LLLIIISSSAAA! finally came out of his mouth, steam shot straight out both ears as he went flying past me and out the door! He picked up the shovel, pitched sawdust in a stall in record time! He went on to the next pile and the next! As I watched, he was putting all that angry energy to work. My heart came back off the floor followed by a massive feeling of relief. I thought, "HE LIVES!" I laughed and jumped for joy at my good fortune. It became my lucky day. Not only did I not kill him, nor he kill me, but he finished bedding all the stalls. I knew my relief laughter was not what he thought. One thing for sure, I never doused him with water, but then again, he never napped on bedding day. What a good lesson!

Another time, I went for a routine doctor visit, back in the day when you sat for hours before you finally got to see the doctor. When the appointment was finally over, I drove to work arriving around 3:30 in the afternoon, feeding time. Quitting time was at 4:00. I should have called it a day, but I thought I would help feed.

As soon as I walked into the barn, my boss was walking out of the stall with an ordinary black horse he had purchased from the auction. I never liked this horse because there was nothing special about him other than the fact he was black. Buying performance horses by color was never a good idea. The horse was not very pretty, nor did he have much talent, and my boss was determined to prove me wrong. He knew how I felt about the horse, and I could always find something more pertinent to do than work that horse.

I walked into the barn to feed, and my boss said, "Hey, come ride this horse. I've been working him, and I want to see what he looks like."

"I don't want to ride that horse. It's quittin' time, and I'm here to help feed," I replied.

"Awww, come on. Ride him, ride him. I want to see what he looks like," he said.

The barn had an asphalt aisle way with stalls on each side. The aisle ran parallel to the aisle way with doors to the outside on each end. On each end of the barn aisle way was a connection to the arena with the broader opening closer to the front of the barn. Reluctantly, I crawled up on that black horse I didn't want to ride, went into the arena and turned to the left. The outside door on the far end was opened which it had not been in the days prior. The horse was startled by this new site and stopped suddenly. I was giving him a moment to take in the new site. To my boss, the horse was backing up.

"He's backing up, he's backing up!" my boss shouted.

CRACK!!! The drop lash whip landed across his hocks to send him forward.

The lick sent him forward like a bullet! The horse lunged, and it wasn't anything I wasn't capable of riding; the problem was I wasn't mentally ready for three seconds of quick thinking. I didn't even want to be on the horse in the first place. When I started to lose my balance, I didn't bother to regain it because I didn't think coming off was going to be any big deal. Unbothered by hitting the ground, I didn't take the fall as I should have and rolled. Instead, I put my arms back to catch myself and hop back on my feet. I hit with more momentum than I had judged. When I brought my left arm around in front of me, I could see it was at a forty-five-degree angle about one inch above my wrist.

I had broken my arm.

If you had ever heard of "Bite the Dust Club," that was how you joined; although, it was not necessary to break something. This was not my first initiation, but one of the most memorable. There was a little burn when my arm broke but, amazingly, it didn't hurt. I sat in the dust disgusted with the new angle of my arm, so I straightened it. Now my arm had a U look to it. I didn't like that view either, but a slight improvement. My boss was in a stir, chasing the loose horse.

"Are you all right?" he yelled.

"I broke my arm," I replied.

"Run down there to the other end and head the horse off!" he coached.

I couldn't believe what I just heard, as a matter of fact, my first thought was "A**HOLE." But I rose up out the dirt, walked around the corner, cradling my broken arm with my other hand, stood in the aisle way and headed the horse off, into his stall. My boss was not far behind, flustered, with his shirt tail hanging out. He ran into the stall to secure the horse.

I stood in the aisle way watching the fiasco play out, dust all over my backside, holding my wrist. My boss ran over with a sick look on his face and started to touch my arm.

"Let me see it," he said.

I had on a long sleeve sweatshirt and brown cotton gloves. He started to pull at my shirt sleeve.

"DON'T TOUCH IT! It doesn't hurt right now, and I want to go to the hospital, and I want to go NOW," I said.

He said he had to run to the house to tell his wife.

"NO YOU DON'T. WE'RE GOING RIGHT NOW! You can call your wife from the hospital!" I demanded.

I felt as if he crossed me at that moment, I would knock his lights out. I still had one good arm!

On the speedy way to the hospital, he was still flustered.

"You're awful calm," he said.

"Well maybe I'm in shock because right now it doesn't hurt, and I know it's going to," I said.

We went to the hospital emergency room, and I walked in on my own power. They met me with a gurney, and I laid on it with my upper torso elevated. There was sawdust on the clean sheets and a trail of dust everywhere I had been. The doctor took an x-ray and showed me what he called a greenstick break. It looked exactly like a jagged, frayed greenstick after breaking one in half. With his hands on each side of my wrist, he took his thumbs to set it back in place. At the moment of setting, the sound of the pop and crack of the bone going back in place would make anyone winch, but luckily, it still didn't hurt. I wished I had thought about giving my boss a silver bullet to bite on because he was squeezing my right arm to death.

My head whirled around, and I said, "LET GO! You're hurting my good arm!" He let go. He looked sick.

You could blame my boss for knocking the horse out from under me. You could blame the horse for stopping or blame me for showing up. But all in all, this was the definition of SH** HAPPENS!

The cast was from my knuckles to above my elbow. The doctor set my wrist at a forty-five-degree angle and my elbow at ninety degrees. I left the hospital with a sling supported with a nylon strap behind my neck. The doctor gave me Tylenol 3 for the pain. That evening, my fingers began to hurt like I never imagined. Why my fingers? I guess all those nerves ended in my fingers and, UGH! did it hurt. Tylenol 3 helped as much as a sugar cube would. The nylon strap on the sling around my neck felt as if it would soon just cut my head off. If that wasn't enough, add every day was a bad hair day because it was impossible to keep up long hair with only one hand. A week earlier, I had just signed up and paid for ten guitar lessons. I wasn't going to give in and went to one. My hand didn't work enough even to grasp the guitar, let alone chord the strings. That was a useless cause.

I considered all this a set back, but I was far from beaten. I was determined to figure out a way to relieve some of this burden. A fireman friend of mine went back to my doctor and talked him into the next level of pain relief. Sometimes during the day, the pain would subside a little, but most of the time, my fingers hurt like h*ll. One pill helped a little for a few days, and then I upped it to two. After a few days, that didn't help, so I added a shot of Kentucky bourbon. A couple of times and then that didn't even work. All the painkillers did was to make my mind feel fuzzy, yet the pain was still there. I finally decided to tolerate the pain. It lasted about six weeks.

The nylon strap behind my neck was the first thing that had to go. I went to the store and bought three different pieces of material, one square yard each, and tied a cravat sling I had learned from a first aid class. It felt like a pillow behind my neck compared to the nylon strap, not to mention the fashion statement. I bought plaids and solids to accessorize my blue jeans and boots ensemble I wore to the barn. My favorite was a blue and black plaid. Maybe it symbolized the black and blue pain I experienced. No, I think I just liked the blue and black plaid material. I doubt we would make the cover of a fashion magazine.

Bad hair days were solved with hair ties with little plastic balls on each end. I could work those with one hand and put my hair in a ponytail. I had just grown my hair out long enough to French braid, an impossible feat with only one hand. I couldn't use the curling iron either, but at least, it went from bad hair days to little better hair days. That was the best I could do. My mom and dad came to visit, and usually, we did fun things, but this time I wanted my mom to help fold my laundry and put clean sheets on the bed. She tried to talk me into coming home, but at least I had something to do by going to work and doing limited things.

Limited things were more than my boss expected. I could feed, water, groom, clean stalls, sweep, saddle and put chains on the horse's feet for work. I couldn't ride, which was my job and carrying water was no fun at all. Why we couldn't pull a hose to each stall, I'll never know. We carried water twice a day and more if the horse was extra thirsty. He wouldn't leave the bucket in the stall, so the horse would have free choice of water. Unavailable water was a constant sore spot with me, but he was the boss. When he ticked me off, and there was an argument, I made sure I picked this point among whatever else I felt was for a horse's welfare and for my own too. Two five-gallon buckets of water were more comfortable to carry than one, because one in each hand balanced the load. One bucket was about forty pounds, and two was eighty. Now, one was all I could carry, holding my broken arm up, while the forty-pound bucket pulled the other arm down. Had I never been measured for a tailored riding suit, I would have never known one shoulder was one inch higher than the other.

One day, I had the job of quieting a young thoroughbred for the farrier to shoe. We were teaching the colt to ride for a neighbor to send to the racetrack. I was holding a lead shank with the chain across the colt's nose to get his attention if I needed it. He was busy and a little too antsy to stand still. After asking and asking to hold still, I decided I needed to get his attention by snatching the chain across his nose. I gave the chain a quick jerk with my right hand only to experience the bones jarring together in my left arm. It made me sick to my stomach.

I bet the color drained out of my face. I quickly passed the colt off to the closest person. I needed to sit down. That was the last time for several weeks I held a horse.

Makes me sick to think about it.

After four and a half weeks, I went back to the doctor. He removed the cast only to replace it with a smaller one. Now my wrist was straight, and the cast ended below my elbow. No more sling! YAY! I could even work with my hair! No more bad hair days! I was back to work for about a week when my boss had to drive to North Carolina for a crisis with his sister. On his way back home, just a few miles into the trip, he realized he was having a heart attack. He drove to the hospital. While he was in the facility, I was in the barn taking care of TEN horses with one arm. If he survived, I would kill him! I fed, carried water, cleaned and bedded stalls, drove the tractor, emptied the manure spreader, climbed into the loft to throw hay down, groomed and walked horses. I was going to kill him, if it was the last thing I ever did!

My saving grace was old man Busch. He started to come by to check on things. He was a local farmer who raised a Saddlebred or two, and we were working his filly. I guess Mr. Busch was probably in his upper seventies at the time. He was soft spoken and never said anything unless you asked him a question or if he had something important to say. I liked Mr. Busch, and he liked me.

He stopped by one day.

"Mr. Busch, I need some sawdust. I know where the sawmill is in Danville, but I don't know how to drive the old truck. Would you drive me?" I asked.

His eyes twinkled as he grinned and nodded yes. The next day after morning chores, we set off on our big adventure. The Danville sawmill destination was about an hour away. It was a very nice sunny day for a drive, and when we were almost there, we pulled into a convenience store and the truck died. No matter what, it wouldn't start up again.

My boss told me the truck might quit, and let it cool, it would start up again. Mr. Busch tried it and tried it, and it wouldn't start.

We got out of the truck, and I looked over at Mr. Busch.

"Let's go right here to this restaurant and have lunch, let the truck cool and hope it starts up. What a pain." I said.

I no sooner had finished that statement when the manager appeared.

"Ma'am, you **have to move your truck.** It's right in front of my store, and it can't be parked here," the manager said.

Well, DUH! Talk about sticking a finger in a sore spot! He was at least twice my size, and I squared off in front of him.

"**Mister**, I would be **so happy** to move my truck from in front of your store, but it just **won't start.** The best I can do is let it cool down and it will start. So, we're going over here to have lunch and let it cool. And then I'll move it. I'm sorry, but that's the best I can do," I said.

He gave me a grimacing look, locked his jaw and stressed his neck. He looked like he wanted to choke me. I was a little indifferent to him, he was the least of my problems. The whole time this was going on, out of the corner of my eye, I could see Mr. Busch. As I spoke to the manager, Mr. Busch took one step back, and his eyes opened wide. I think he was doing his best to choke back a smile. It wasn't until we sat down to eat that he let out a laugh. When my boss eventually got back, Mr. Busch couldn't wait to tell him what "that little woman" did. If you think old women cackle, you should hear old men!

After lunch, fortunately, the old truck did start, but just long enough to get across the street to a real gas station. Mr. Busch and I combined resources to pay to have it fixed so we could finish our task and get home. The next day, Mr. Busch showed up again. I think he enjoyed the adventure.

"Mr. Busch, I could ride these horses, but I can't get on. If you help hold them beside this trunk, I'll get on," I said.

So that's what we did. I held the left rein between my fingers, and the cast, and reset my grip at the end of every straightaway pass. At least the horses were now exercised more than just hand walked.

My boss finally returned from his hospital stay. I let him live, and work got back to normal. I got my second cast off, a total of eight and a half weeks had passed. My arm had atrophied and looked pitiful. My wrist could only bend the way it was set in the cast, forty-five degrees to straight. I was afraid to work with it. Thanksgiving week came, and I drove home to visit, and gave my arm a rest without the cast. No one mentioned physical therapy. I devised a method to get my arm to work as it did before the break. Without knowing what I was doing, someone would have thought I was doing some weird praying ritual. Who cared, it worked. Eventually, my arm was as good as new.

Months later, Mr. Busch invited my boss and me to come to his house. He had something he wanted to show us. I made a point to go. I met his wife who was very sweet, and their home was warm and inviting. He took us to the connected garage, and there was a late 1920's Studebaker his dad purchased brand new. He courted his wife in the car and garaged it soon after. The car was all original and in showroom shape. I had never seen such a well-cared for relic up close before. The car was green with a stained wood steering wheel and wooden spoked wheels. All the seats were the original crushed velvet with special interior luxury appointments. Not a GPS, but a bud vase mounted in the back on the side and another one mounted on the front of the dash, not on top, to keep the rose from wilting in the sun. Mr. Busch raised the hood to make an adjustment and proceeded to crank it up for us. I looked at the car with amazement and looked over at Mr. Busch. There he was with that twinkle in his eye and the grin little boys have when they finally let you in on their secret. To this day, I love to see classic cars and the pride owners take in them.

Ten years later, my husband and I were in Kentucky, and he loved old cars. I told him all about Mr. Busch's treasure, and we decided to call him to see if he would show us his car. I called a friend to get his number, and she informed me that his wife had died a few years back. He answered the door and invited us in. The house now had that bachelor look. My husband was as thrilled as I was when I first saw the antique car. But the TLC of the vehicle was gone, still magnificent, yet carried years of dust. After a short admiration of the car, we thanked Mr. Busch and left. It broke my heart to see the twinkle in his eye, gone. I guess the light of his life left this earth before he did.

If it weren't for the mutual love of the Saddlebred horse, our paths would have never crossed. I thank God for that. If it hadn't been for a broken arm and a heart attack, there would have never been an adventure with Mr. Busch. Funny how life works.

Before my boss died, he came to visit in Virginia to see one of my horses work. I let him to stay in our camper parked at the barn. It was early spring and sometimes the temperature swings can be twenty to thirty degrees. It was a nice seventy-degree day when I left him, and I showed him the camper comforts, but it never occurred to me to close the ceiling vents. Any heat went out the top. I came into the barn the next day and he was sitting on the bench shivering and looking pitiful.

"I almost froze to death in that camper last night. I've never been so cold," he said.

"Well, now that you are diabetic, you will understand what I am about to say. Do you remember that day when you refused to buy me a honey bun and my sugar dropped through the floor?" I asked.

"Oh, my God," he muttered.

"I couldn't care less that you almost froze last night, 'cause PAYBACKS are H*LL!" I chuckled.

What goes around, comes around. Time always catches up.

IV

Stumbling into a Pit of Horror

11

Feeling of Sadness

I was glad when the good memories of Mark replaced the grief and guilt. I was beginning to get back to work at the barn, and one day while I was working alone with my thoughts, I was thinking of Mark. I hoped it was the last lingering feeling of sadness. And that was okay. It was a sunny, very still day and even though it was a beautiful day, I just couldn't seem to shake my black cloud. I knew if I would let the sadness out, it would pass right through and be gone.

Around lunchtime, hunger began to set in, and I drove to the gas station, Race-In, which had a neat little cafe inside, and was one of my favorite lunch spots. A lot of working locals had decided the same thing. It was our meeting place.

I entered the cafe with the longest face in the world. An old friend, Debbie, saw me and as I caught her eye, her eyes widened, and her face showed great worry. I guessed she had never seen me with such a long face before.

"LISA...Are you okay...?" she asked.

"Yeah," was my weak reply. We had shared stories of lost animals, a couple of months before in the same cafe, so I knew she knew my horse loss.

Her entire family was with her. With their reaction, it was obvious to everyone that I was not of normal character.

What was so interesting to me was that friends don't like seeing friends sad any more than I liked being sad. They immediately started trying to pick me up. Somehow, we got into sharing stories of visiting out west. Everyone knows laughter is the best medicine, so when we shared a laugh, they looked happy when it appeared they had succeeded in cheering me up. Soon, they got up to leave. It took less than a minute for my feeling of deep sadness to come back and Debbie, of course, didn't miss it and came closer.

"Lisa, have you seen a doctor? Maybe he could give you something to help," she said.

"Debbie....do I really need a doctor to tell me I have a broken heart?" I said.

No... I guess not," she said with relief.

I know there's not a pill for everything that ails me. The only way to get past this sadness and grief is to feel what I feel, and it will eventually change. Just like the weather, no matter how severe, it always changes. I've never seen a big black cloud blow in and NEVER blow back out again. I have met people who seemed to have a string tied around their black cloud, and everywhere they go, their black cloud goes with them. I've known other people who won't slow down long enough to let their black cloud catch up. If they only knew, it would pass on through if they would stop running. Gladly, by the end of the day, the feeling of sadness passed on, and that's what I had hoped. My black cloud had finally passed, and blue skies appeared.

Grief is not something to get "over," it is something one has to go "through." "Just get over it," is an insensitive statement.

Three years later, I saw my friend, Debbie, at The Race In. We chatted a few minutes, and she finally opened up.

"Did I tell you I lost my David?" she said.

"No," I replied.

She went on to say she lost her husband David and her dad all in the same year. I went over and stood silently beside her while she told of her grief. She stopped after a while and looked at me.

"Well, you know I know a little about grief. My method of dealing with it is to take a swan dive in the middle of it, as to get to the bottom as fast as I can because it takes hitting bottom before I can come up the other side. When all that hurt goes away, then the good times start to come back," I said.

"Funny you should say that. Just last week I began to want to visit my daughter. I went and actually had fun," she said.

"Oh, how wonderful! You are beginning on the way up. But be aware, it is not a straight line. In time, if you work in the direction of climbing up, you will be left with the happy memories, and the pain will be gone," I said.

"Yes, that will be great," she said.

"Well, now do you think a pill can fix a broken heart?" I asked.

"No," she quickly agreed.

Similar experiences lead to understanding. A good listener is a treasure.

12

Website and Sign

I was riding high from our wonderful family trip out west, yet I still carried one worry. Would I defend myself and my work in the future if someone tried to take it over, or tell me what to do with it, or would I be just too polite and afraid I might make someone mad if I did? It was amazing how fast the test came.

Two years earlier, the preacher and I had agreed on developing a website. I would design and get the site working, and he would supply the copy. I had done my part of the job, the site was up and running, but the it was never finished.

I was catching up on emails after the trip, and I received one from a church member that read something like this: "Hi Lisa, I have volunteered to take over the website. I have experience with website design and..."

I thought, "Takeover--TAKEOVER--ARE YOU KIDDING ME?!" It launched me up and out of my recliner and then my feet finally hit the floor. I had enough gusto to take on any Sumo wrestler and flatten him with my bare hands. It took a few minutes for me to land back on earth. Why had this upset me so?

In a couple of days, when I completely got my feet back on the ground, I replied to the email. "...I am glad you are interested in the website. I welcome your help on its development, and I would be glad for you to join the committee. Thank you for your interest, but it is not available for takeover. I look forward to working with you..."

I phoned the preacher and told him of the takeover email I received and laughed about it helping to lay my last worry to rest. I laughed. I won.

"Good news, the website has gotten in two new families, and one of them is a marketing manager from Charlotte and he can... also, as you know, another member has taught website design and he can...." he said.

Was I not hearing this right? Why was it all about what the "great white men" could do? Why did I feel like all the men wanted was to take over my website work? Not one person asked me what I had done or where we were in the process. The website was not finished because copy had yet to be supplied. The preacher and I had been touching base over the last two years and every time I asked for copy, there was a crisis, or one of us was out of town. Each page said, "Under Construction." I put together such a good design, it still got families into the church. Why was I getting the blame for the website not being finished?

I took a stand on defending **my** work, and for the very first time in my life, I quoted credentials.

"Well, if credentials are what you want, I will tell you. I graduated with a bachelor's in art, Cum Laude I might add. I have done national advertising in this country and Europe. I've designed national logos, ad campaigns, magazine covers, thoroughbred sales catalog covers, sold photographs for advertising, painted an oil which was purchased and hangs in the home of a Hollywood star, a pastel that hangs in the home of a multi-million-dollar entertainment enterprise, to name a few. Specifically, for the website, I purchased the domain name and hosting for the church's website, and I designed it as we discussed to be consistent with the newsletter. The site was fourteen pages long. After I designed it all with the rock background to match the newsletter, the website took five minutes to load. No one is going to wait that long. I had to take the site down and redesign, so it would download quicker...all fourteen pages. If you click on a page, it goes to that page, if you click on another one, it goes to that one too. All fourteen pages work. And if two families found it, I did that too. Just because you put a website up doesn't mean Google and other search engines will find it. You can either pay for that service or, since I know how it works, I set that service up myself. I did such a good job because it is the first church website to come up when anyone googles a church in our town. So that's what I've done," I said.

Silence..."Oh, I didn't know that," he said, and he quietly added, "Well, I told them it wasn't your fault it wasn't finished." Then why was everyone wanting to takeover my work?

On Saturday, I was walking into the Wellness Center to swim. I saw a childhood friend on his way out, and I could tell he wanted to talk. We sat down on the brick wall outside the Center and began to chat. He is a courtroom judge, and we had been friends since we were kids. When I was eight-years-old, Mom took me to his mother's farm for horseback riding lessons. I had started riding at six, but my instructor left for school. His mother set me up with a teenage neighbor to teach me to ride horses. I went to his home at least twice a week for two years for lessons. They treated me as one of their family.

We started the chat by asking about each other's moms. The conversation went on to the church, where we were both members and the church was across the street from his house. I had been a member of this church all my life except for nine years when I lived in Kentucky. I always referred to it as Granddaddy's church. It was special to me. My childhood friend and his family had recently been members but left because of the controversy with an LED sign the church wanted to put up.

"Do you know if they are going to put up the LED sign?" he asked.

"I don't know. I've been out of town and before that I wasn't participating due to the loss of my horse," I replied.

"The preacher had the church rezoned to commercial and changed the sign ordinance, so the church could put up a lighted sign they wanted. The sign ordinance was put in place, so our town would grow into a quaint, inviting town tourists would like to visit. Undoing the law will, in time, take away the look the forefathers had envisioned for the town," he said very concerned.

"I agree with you. I've just been to Sedona, Arizona, and it must even have a building ordinance for how lovely everything went with the landscape. I know what you're talking about," I said.

"I've wanted to talk to someone in your family because it was your little brother who invited me to Vacation Bible School when I was a kid and I wanted my kids to go there because it felt like my church family. I go to another church now, and it is all right, but it's just not the same" he said. I could see his pain due to the loss of his church family.

"You know Lisa, the preacher went around and talked to all the neighbors about what the church wanted to do, but he never walked across the street and discussed it with me. The discussion ended up in a town council meeting, and it got very personal," he said.

"Wow. Ok, I've got a meeting coming up with him about the church website, I will find out about the sign. I'm glad I ran into you, and I'll let you know what I find out. Take care, and I'm going to swim," I replied. He thanked me, and he seemed relieved to talk to someone who really listened.

I thought about the conversation while I swam. I decided I would work up through the channels and that would be a better approach than a public, personal fight. I thought since I was the only granddaughter of one of the most beloved preachers of that church, they might listen to what I had to say. And after all, I could design a hundred different signs. I'm sure it could be worked out, and all would be happy. It just needed a different point of view.

A day or two after, I had lunch with my mom.

"Do you know if they are putting up an LED sign at the church?" I asked.

"I don't know, I've been traveling like you. I'm not on that committee, but I hope not. Don't ask your brother," she instructed.

My brother is on the Session, the governing body of our church. That's why I wanted to talk to him. Mom knows I can make him madder than anyone here on earth. He gets mad at me whenever I don't agree with him or if I'm in the way of something he wants. Whenever he gets mad at me, I get blamed. It has been like that all my life. I think he is mad at me for being born, so how can I help that? He picked on me so often growing up; his middle name became Quit. He would push my button, and I would get irritated and fuss. When I got in trouble, he would gloat. Sometimes he would get in trouble, I would be satisfied. What good is a sibling if you can't fight with them once in a while?

I felt entirely different about him than he thought about me. I thought it was nice to have not just one, but two big brothers. I thought big brothers were supposed to protect little sisters. One was a protector and I needed to be protected from the other one. Sometimes, I did goad him for the fun of it. Aren't I a good sister?

I didn't pay any attention to what my mom said. We were all adults, and I wanted to talk to someone on the Session, and why not my brother? It was his granddaddy's church too.

I called my brother and his wife answered the phone. "Hello?"

"I would like to talk to my brother about the sign. The judge talked to me outside the Wellness Center, and I would like to hear what went on in the town council meeting." I said.

"Well if it has to do with the judge, he doesn't want to talk to you," she said.

"That's okay, I'll ask another session member. Thanks. Bye," I said.

In a couple of minutes, she called back.

"Ok, he said come over at seven," she said. I agreed.

I went to his house at seven that evening. We sat down in the living room and talked about my trip, some of the places we went, how much fun it was and how I had found closure to losing Mark. I also told him about finally getting to work on the website. He asked me if I would be head of the committee to oversee the site.

"Sure, I would love to," I said. I was excited with the opportunity.

Then I asked him what went on at the town council meeting. He became very agitated telling me his version. He said it got very personal and the preacher took the high road, and the judge didn't even know the law. I'm thinking to myself, a doctor and a preacher think the judge doesn't know the law? What planet are they from or am I the one who has lost my mind? I just thought I lost my horse. My brother got a little more heated with the description of the town meeting. Now I'm thinking; "I know which side got personal and it wasn't the judge." I very politely tried to tell my point of view using Sedona as the example, and he attacked me for taking the judge's side.

"Sides?" I said, "I want to discuss the facts. It has nothing to do with sides." He was mad, but I'm used to it.

I proceeded to ask my sister-in-law "What do you think of the LED sign?"

"Well, I don't like it, but I'm supporting the preacher," she said.

My brother wouldn't say if he liked the sign or not, but he was supporting the preacher. In my next attempt to speak, my brother interrupted, and I couldn't get a word in edgewise as he told me how narrow-minded I was. I thought, I'd heard his side, my sister-in-law's side, Mom's side, the judge's side, and I'm narrow-minded? I don't even look at it as sides. Point of view would be a much better description; therefore, no one has to take sides and team up against the other. Instead of win or lose, everyone would be right; therefore, everyone wins.

I learned what I wanted from this visit, which was what happened during the town council meeting, and tried to get him to see the mistake our church had made. I realized our beloved church had taken a prior member, a respected, upstanding person in the community, and flogged him in public. One comment I got from the meeting was one person said, "Why couldn't the church spend the money to help the people of the community instead of spending it on an expensive sign." Frankly, I agreed with him. I don't like to see churches spend their money outside the community, and that was where most of the sign money was going... outside the town. When I stood up to leave and say one last thing, my brother heatedly cut me off and said he had work to do.

I finally raised my voice and said firmly, "Hey, if you build this sign, YOU WILL DRIVE A STAKE THROUGH THE MIDDLE OF HILLSVILLE!!!"

He scoffed and went one way, I shrugged and went the other. We ended up talking on the phone that night, mostly about the website. I quietly reiterated I thought the purpose of the sign was to bring more people into the church and if you alienate the community, how were you going to do that?

"I hear what you're saying," he said softly.

In my eyes, God had sent us a sign, but I felt like I was the only one that could read it. "Love thy neighbor as thyself." Why could no one else see it?

The pain this sign had brought was becoming more apparent to me, and I knew the judge's mother very well. I knew she would be upset. She took me in as one of her own whenever I was at their house as a child. I have fond memories of making taffy, pulling and stretching the candy to get it to the right consistency. She included me in on her bright idea of creating a parade float out of a pony cart. We spent hours laughing and stuffing tissue paper in the chicken wire to decorate the float. She took us to the parade, plus the pony and cart, and it was excellent childhood fun. I did the same thing with my son when he was about four with my pony and cart, without the tissue paper, and my husband bought us a giant bag of candy to throw out all down the parade route. She was at the parade, cheering as we passed. I gave her thumbs up with the biggest smile!

I called her to apologize for the pain the church had caused. She was so upset the sign episode might have hurt her son's reputation. Moms are protective. I tried to assure her that his reputation was stronger than the sign.

"Well, I can design a hundred different signs if necessary. I'm sure we can come up with an alternative," I said.

"I don't know why the sign is that important, I thought the steeple on top of the church told everybody what the church was all about. Why do you need a sign? This will never be undone," she said.

"Well, maybe not, if no one tries, it won't be. I'm just calling you to tell you I am going to try," I said. She thanked me and seemed a little relieved.

I went to church on Sunday, and I was glowing with peace within me from finally getting over the grief of my horse. I marched up across the lawn and caught the ladies' eyes who were standing and talking. They did a double take when they saw how I was beaming. That day came up in conversation with one of them on a later Sunday, and I said how good I felt after the trip.

"Oh, I saw you, YOU WERE GLOWING!" one lady said.

I smiled at the thought. On my way out the door after the sermon was over, the preacher and I joked with each other as usual. He had asked to meet with me concerning the site, before I went on our trip.

"When do you want to get together about the website?" I asked.

"Thursday morning and I might have a lunch date," he said.

"Ok, I'll see you then," I said, and I left.

I called him later to tell him of my plan for the website and see if it suited him.

"Well if you don't mind, I'm going to talk to other members of the church to get their input on the website because this will be our image. The website will be our image, kind of like a logo. When I designed logos before, I would interview the business owner and let them describe how they wanted their business represented. Then I created a graphic image based on their description. This website is a little different because I am in the church and the image was created from my viewpoint. I think I should get more input because it is everybody's church. When everybody has their input, I will give it to the church," I said. He said it sounds good and talk to anyone I wanted.

I only had time to speak to one person before the meeting, and he knows every aspect of the church. I learned many things I didn't know. He was concerned because the numbers were going down and down in many mainstream churches. He said in our church, if things keep going the way they were going, in ten years, we could only afford a part-time minister. I asked him about the sign, and the judge's name came up. He took the opposing "side" and even said, "yeah, the judge even wanted flowers." I thought, "What is wrong with flowers! NOTHING!" If the judge wanted it, they were against it. This situation was becoming a lot harder than I thought, but surely the voice of reason would eventually be heard. I'll work up through the correct channels.

Thursday rolled around, and I showed up at the meeting with the preacher around 9:30. I wasn't back to work yet, and for the first time, I felt like what it would be like to be retired and to spend my time however I wanted. I thought it was terrific to be chatting with a friend. I started with my trip and the fun we had, and then I mentioned my horse. The conversation turned to the sign.

"So, I hear you are getting your sign," I said.

"It isn't my sign," he said.

Puzzled, "Well, whose is it?" I asked.

"It's the church's," he replied.

I thought as far as the LED sign; Mom hoped not, my sister-in-law didn't like it, my brother wouldn't say, and the preacher wouldn't claim it. Why put up a sign and cause such hard feelings? Is this how our government works?

"Well, I would like to propose another option," I suggested.

"Too late, the decision has already been made," he said.

"It's just a decision. It is not like the trees that have already been cut down, and you can't put them back up, or a constructed sign that has already been built and you can't take it down. A decision can be changed," I said.

"Well, if that's what you want to do, you have to have a written proposal to the session before the next meeting, and you will be put on the agenda, and then you present it in person," he said.

I agreed. I looked at my watch, and it was 11:30.

"Don't you have a lunch date?" I asked.

He scrunched his face, shook his head no and didn't budge from his chair.

The conversation continued, and since I was head of the website committee, I had questions how the committee worked. I needed clarification on the governing rules. One question led to another and another and another. Finally, I started asking about the sign and why he talked to everyone else in the neighborhood, but not the judge.

"Well the judge didn't come talk to me," he said.

"Isn't that your job to reach out?" I asked.

The more we talked, the less I liked the answers. I had slowly started to melt down in my chair.

"I did my job, why didn't you do yours?" I asked.

I didn't want to hear his answer. I wanted him to think about it awhile. I glanced down at my watch.

"Oh my gosh! It's 1:30! I gotta go!" I exclaimed. And swoosh! Out the door, I went!

13

All Hell Broke Loose

The next morning, I received a voicemail from the preacher politely asking me to return his call. I phoned him and identified myself. I was shocked when he started yelling at me.

"LISA, I'VE BEEN THINKING ABOUT OUR FIVE HOUR CONVERSATION. IN FACT, I WAS AWAKE MOST OF THE NIGHT THINKING ABOUT IT. AND I'M GONNA BE HEAD OF THE WEBSITE COMMITTEE, AND YOU ARE GONNA BE ON THE COMMITTEE. YOU ARE GONNA TELL ME HOW MUCH THE CHURCH OWES YOU FOR THE DOMAIN NAME, THE HOSTING AND YOUR TIME, BECAUSE IF IT'S THE CHURCH'S WEBSITE, THE CHURCH NEEDS TO OWN IT!" he yelled.

It was 8:30 in the morning and the preacher was screaming at me!

"Ok, I'm GLAD you finally decided TO LEAD, and I will HELP you! But you should know, if things keep going the way they are going, we can't afford a full-time minister; therefore, I'll have to dig deeper into my pocket TO PAY YOUR SALARY!" I snapped.

Both of us sharply hung up! What was wrong with him, screaming at me so early this morning?

It took me less than five seconds to know **that didn't go right**.

In another minute, I texted him.

"I didn't like the tone of our conversation, let's have a do-over."

"Yes, I think we need to talk, but I need some time to think," he texted back.

"Take all the time you need; you are worth the wait," I texted back.

The next day, my mom came over to the barn. I was happily working along and didn't think much about what had happened with the preacher because I thought the we were on the way to working it out.

"Lisa, you have made the preacher mad. He said you TOOK five hours of his time," Mom said.

"I don't think it was that long. So?" I replied.

"He was so mad he was going to quit. What did you say to him?" Mom asked.

"Well, mostly I asked questions. What's wrong with that?" I asked.

"Well nothing is wrong with questions. But you TOOK five hours of his time!" she said.

"Mom, he GAVE five hours of his time, and what, now he wants it BACK?" I chuckled.

"Well, you said something that made him mad. You know, I think you are still grieving over your horse, and you need a grief counselor," she said.

"Mom, I'm already over my horse. That's what I have been doing for the past five months and taking a trip out west was just the icing on the cake for me to get over it. I'm over it, and I'm glad," I said.

"Well, you need a grief counselor," she said.

I chuckled again and went on about my work. Mom frustrated not getting the answers she wanted, she left.

The next day, she came back and hounded me about a grief counselor.

"Mom, I've already talked to a grief counselor, George. I saw him in June at Blowing Rock. He said I was doing the right thing. I don't need a grief counselor. I'm past it," I said.

"Oh, George. I like him. Let's call him," she said.

"Well, if YOU need a grief counselor, go ahead," I said.

"No, you call him," she said.

"No Mom, I don't need a grief counselor. I've already talked to him," I said.

She was frustrated with me again and left. I found humor in the whole thing, but she wouldn't take no for an answer. I knew I wasn't to blame for the preacher being mad, some, granted, but not like they were trying to pin on me. I began to laugh and played the game of giving her everything she wanted except control over me.

She called me the next day and said, "Well I think I'll call George, what's his number."

"I don't know. Get on the Saddlebred website and put his name in as a member and see if it comes up." I was amused.

"Oh no. George works for a church in Roanoke, I'll call them," she said.

"Great! You do that!" I said.

I thought she would get George and he would tell her the same thing I told her, and I would be done with this nonsense. She called, and the secretary quoted the HIPAA rule which said they couldn't give out any of that information. I hadn't talked to him as a professional. I spoke to him as a friend. I was disappointed with the response, but really, I was fifty-three years old. I guess it was none of mom's business.

I was busy trying to write and jump through all the hoops necessary to make a new sign proposal. I didn't need this craziness. I found humor in the situation that had blown up so way out of proportion. I thought at the time the whole fiasco was utterly ridiculous! I laughed, I won. Or so I thought.

Finally, my mother called me and asked me to lunch. I met her at a Mexican restaurant. I was definitely on a different plain from everyone else because my happiness from finding peace was with me every day, and I was so incredibly happy! Mom was still very serious about my run-in with the preacher. I thought it was just a misunderstanding, not a big deal, and he and I would work it out. She kept hounding me about the blowup and that I needed a grief counselor. I laughed at the drama, and I just thought I could get the preacher to realize a sign wasn't worth losing a member, a neighbor, my childhood friend when I could design many alternatives. Unfortunately, I didn't say that to my mom that clearly. With a huge smile, I said, "Mom, I have seen the light!"

And before I could get out the explanation, she interrupted me.

"Lisa, you are not the savior of our church," she said. Then she leaned across the table and her next comment sent me into orbit! "Lisa, you need a doctor," she said.

At that very moment, I no longer thought any of this was funny. I WAS HORRIFIED! Deep from within my subconscious, a happening from twenty-five years ago came roaring back at me, when she had said the same thing! "Lisa, you need a doctor." This was a MAJOR BREAKTHROUGH! I knew there was nothing wrong with me now and I realized, there was NOTHING WRONG WITH ME then! For twenty-five years, I had carried a false shame. I soon realized it wasn't what I had done, but what my mother had done to me!

Oh, my God! My heart is pounding just trying to get this down on paper!

I left the restaurant and as the day went on, the more my anger built up. I had no idea how much suppressed anger I had. Tom and I had problems in our marriage, and he was not at that time, the "go to" person to let my anger erupt.

The next morning, I went over to my girlfriend's house and **exploded** with twenty-five years of built up anger that erupted like a volcano. I was almost yelling at the top of my lungs about what my mother had done to me so long ago. My friend had known my mother for several years and knew her the same as everyone else in the community, as a very kind, caring, sweet, and gracious woman with loads of southern charm. My explosion and the context came as a shock to her.

"Oh, Lisa, I can't believe she did that to you!" she said.

I'll never forget the look on my friend's face, and I bet she can say the same about me. I stood on one side of the kitchen, and she stood on the other with the island in between. It served as a barrier. My explosion was enormous! It was not aimed at her. I just needed a place to unload! After all those years of pent-up anger, I had to LET IT OUT! It was another huge turning point in my life.

I thank God for my friend. What would I had done without her?!

14

Twenty-five Years Ago

I was working in Kentucky as an assistant horse trainer. I had met the man of my dreams. He was a young, good-looking veterinarian with a string of girlfriends. I met him at the barn where I was working, and several times he was called to do minor vet work. He started to appear at the little country church I was attending. One day, I finally got brave enough to invite him to my little cottage for dinner, and he quickly accepted.

The day of our date, he called.

"Lisa, I'm sorry I can't make it. I have an emergency call almost all the way to Richmond, and it will be late when I get back. I don't know how long it will take while I'm there," he said.

"Can I go?" I asked.

"Do you want to?" he asked.

"Well, yeah, I'd love to," I jumped at the chance.

He drove to my rented little cottage and picked me up on his way to the call. We talked and talked all the way there.

It was almost dark by the time we arrived. The horse was lame on one front foot, and the girl owner was anxious and upset. I held the horse with the lead rope in one hand, and the flashlight in the other, assuring the girl her horse would be okay. My prince charming was down on his hands and knees fishing out a giant wooden splinter from the coronet band of the horse's foot. He triumphantly showed us the culprit that had lamed the horse. The owner was grateful for the after-hours trip. He finished by bandaging the horse's foot, and we hopped in his truck and left.

"I sure am glad you were with me. I wouldn't have had any trouble with the horse, but I would have had a hard time dealing with that nutty girl," he said.

I was most amused, and we chatted and chatted all the way back. He said he was sorry about supper and he would take a rain check.

In a couple of weeks, I asked him over for supper again. We made plans a few of days ahead because, professionally, he was in demand.

Again, he called to cancel. "Lisa, this is my only free time in weeks, and I need to get bills out because, in some cases, I am three months behind."

"Bring 'em over if you like, and I'll help," I offered.

"Really? Ok," he said.

We had another evening together. I thought it was great fun to help him and cook a homemade meal. Again, he was very appreciative.

Before I even had the first date with him, the funniest thing happened while he was examining a horse where I worked. One of my girlfriends, who was also friends with my boss and my charming vet, was at the barn. It was one of those sweltering Kentucky days in July, up in the mid-nineties with suffocating humidity. This weather was not like the mountain air of Virginia where I grew up. I wasn't used to the extreme heat and humidity and had become very hot. My friend was holding the horse, while Prince Charming was again crawling around inspecting a horse's foot. I had to do something to cool off. I had the bright idea to grab the bottom of my jeans and pull them up my leg as far as I could. The jeans turned inside out the higher I pulled them. Up went one leg and then the other. It let out several degrees of heat, and I was happy it seemed to work even though it probably looked stupid. Yet, it worked even better than I had planned. Work boots and socks, bare legs a little above the knee, with inside-out jeans. What a picture! My girlfriend looked at me and chuckled, and we both noticed his examination had turned to my legs.

"Why do you have your pants, like that?" he said.

"Because I'M HOT!" I exclaimed.

I didn't realize the double meaning of what I said until it came out. It was all my girlfriend could do to hold a straight face. I doubt if I would have made the cover of a fashion magazine, but I realized the examination of the horse, at that point, was over. He couldn't take his eyes off me. I couldn't help but laugh at myself and the situation, knowing holding a straight face for me was not even an option. The whole blunder worked in my favor. I walked away chuckling, and into the tack room, so his attention could get off me and back on the horse.

I don't remember how many dates before we ended up on my living room floor with the most passionate of kisses. Prince Charming asked to get in that big bed of mine and, truthfully, all I wanted to do was to rip my clothes off. I knew there were other girls in the picture and I didn't just want to be another notch on the bedpost, so I said, "No." I had kissed a lot of toads in my life to find the one man **I wanted**. There were a lot of men who wanted me and a few who asked me to marry. **He** was the one **I wanted.**

I was in love and I thought I was doing a good job reeling him in. He started coming to the same church and I knew it was to see me. One Sunday, I was low on gas and I have a terrible habit of never carrying enough cash. I asked Prince Charming if I could borrow $20 and I would pay him back. He reached in his billfold and handed me a $100 bill. I don't know if that was all he had or if he wanted to impress me. Anyway, it did impress me he would trust me to pay him back, or maybe the money didn't matter. I was on cloud nine, like anyone when they think they are in love.

The dream of landing Prince Charming came to a crashing end when my boss informed me that "the redhead," another woman my prince charming had seen, had gotten pregnant. My heart broke. I never told him how I felt; I never asked him how he felt, I just tried graciously to bow out of the picture, because I thought that was what I was "supposed to do" now that he had other responsibilities. On the rebound, I agreed to marry someone else. Deep down, I knew that was a mistake. He was the greatest of guys, but he felt more like a brother to me than a romantic interest.

As for my work, I finally got sick and tired of my boss sexually harassing me like he had done the entire two years I had worked for him. His emotional abuse "that I would never make it without him" was taking its toll. I finally quit my job. I had handled his harassment, but I had enough of his abuse. I had another job waiting as soon as I was ready to take it.

After church one Sunday, I sat in my little house to think, yet there were no thoughts. I was unable to process anything I felt. I sat for hours with no thought. At the end of that day, I decided I would go home to Virginia for a break. I packed up my clothes and my dog and left.

On the way home to Virginia, I picked up a hitchhiker. He reminded me of my younger brother; both were blonde headed, and the hitchhiker had a Labrador puppy with him. I made a judgment call that he looked to be harmless. I stopped and asked him if he wanted a ride. He got in the car, cradling his puppy in his arms. Both had gray road dirt from head to toe.

"Thank you so much for the picking me up. I have been stranded out on this road for a day and a half, and my boss won't help me. He won't send any money or any help, and I just want to go home. Do you have anything to eat?" he asked.

I reached into my glove compartment and handed him all that I had, a pack of crackers and cheese. He took a bite and gave his puppy a taste. I liked him right away. He lived in Morehead, where I had gone to school, so I was very familiar with his home. I exited off the four-lane and took him right to his front door.

"Would you like to come in for a sandwich?" He said.

I said, "Ok," followed him into his house and sat down at the kitchen table. He fixed me what amounted to a wish sandwich, two slices of bread and wish you had some meat. I think it had mayonnaise, lettuce and maybe pickles. He apologized for it. He then made one for himself, and we sat at the table and had lunch. I told him it was good and thanked him. He thanked me for the ride and off I went, traveling four more hours home.

I was home for about a day, when my grandmother called me to come to her house. She lived two houses up the street. I went straight away, and she asked me if I would paint her kitchen cabinets. I said, "Sure," and began to take off the handles from the doors and drawers as she watched. They were the kind of metal cabinets popular in the fifties with chrome handles. She stood there and chatted with me while I removed all the handles to do a good job.

"Ok, where's the paint?" I asked.

"I don't have it yet," she said.

"Well, when you get the paint you want, call me, and I'll finish the job." I left.

I walked back home thinking that I wanted to talk to Mom, but I didn't know what to say. I didn't know what I was feeling or how to express it. I was taught to control emotions, but I was never taught to understand them. Sometimes I was told "not to feel that way." Suppressing my emotions was how I learned to control them. I did not understand my feelings, and by suppressing them, I wasn't in touch with how I felt. It was damaging not knowing what I felt. It hampered my communication skills.

Instead of talking to Mom, I spent some time with my horses. Another friend asked me to go to West Virginia and see some horses with him. I agreed, and the next day, I drove my car with my dog and a seventy-year-old friend on a journey to see his friend's horses. Little did I know how the trip would take a turn. We left on one of the main roads out of town. It was curvy and up and down hills.

I don't know what made me do this, but I found myself letting the car roll as far as it could downhill until it came to a stop. When the car rolled to a halt, I turned it off, took the keys and my dog, and left my friend standing there hollering, "Where are you going?" I climbed the wire fence and started walking across the cow pasture, looking at the ground, watching where I stepped and never looking up. If I felt like going left, I went left. If I felt like going right, I went right. If a creek got in the way, I jumped it. If a fence showed up, I climbed it. Further and further I walked until finally I stopped and looked up. I had no idea how far I had walked or where I was. I didn't recognize anything. I thought, "I'm lost." I can look back now and see that I acted out what I was feeling. I was lost.

My journey continued as I saw a little brick house. I walked over and knocked on the door. A lady opened the door up and asked if she could help me.

"Can I have a drink of water?" I asked.

She invited me in and welcomed me to her kitchen table. She handed me a drink of water.

"What are you doing out here?" she asked.

"Well--I was going with a friend--to see horses...." I struggled for an answer. I began to come back to my senses and realized in what a ridiculous situation I had put myself.

"I need to go back," I said.

"Where's back?" she asked.

I very clearly told her where my car was, who I was, who my dad was, and he ended up being her dentist. She was pleased to help me.

We got in her car, and she drove where I said my car was located. The scene was a little different than I left it. There was my mom, my friend, my car, and the police. My dog had gone her own way, but don't worry. She was returned home later. I thanked the lady and got out to face the music.

"Hi Mom," I said with a grin as I walked up to her.

She looked horrified. The police saw nothing was hurt, I was fine, no property was damaged, no one was harmed, and they left. My mom kept telling me to come home, and my friend bravely got back in the car with me, and I drove him home and went home myself.

My mom was waiting for me to come home and, immediately, she started in on me.

"Lisa, you're sick, you're sick. You need a doctor."

Sound familiar?

I thought that was utterly ridiculous. "Mom, I'm not sick. Look at me. I've been working ten horses a day. I'm in great physical shape! I'm not sick!"

"You're sick, you're sick, you need a doctor, you need a doctor!" she kept saying, all day. "You're sick, you need a doctor." There seemed to be no way I could convince her.

My grandmother was calling. "Where's Lisa, where's Lisa, she took all the handles off my cabinets. Where's Lisa?" my grandmother kept saying. She never told Mom WHY I took the handles off her cabinets. I guess she got the paint.

She had been on my case all day that I needed a doctor and that I needed to go to the hospital. By night time, my life began to pass before my eyes.

"Mom, I see pictures!" That was true. I think in pictures as many creative people do, and this was nothing new to me.

"Stop saying that!" she said.

She must have thought I was hallucinating. Seeing pictures was normal for me, but I definitely was breaking down from all her badgering. Who wouldn't under those conditions? I'm going to tell you: when you go home to the only place in the world you know to go, it is a scary thing when your mom wants to send you away. Pictures of my life, searching for answers to say to her, started flashing through my sharp mind at record speed.

"STOP THE WORLD, I WANT TO GET OFF!" I demanded!

Now, I understood how people admitted to crimes they didn't commit by being forcefully interrogated all day. I finally agreed to go to the hospital just to shut her up. But I thought I was going to get a physical and I would prove to her I wasn't sick. I didn't need a doctor!

Looking back, I could have made my life so peaceful, if I would have been quiet and simply walked away. I've always heard, "You can never go home." Maybe, "You SHOULD NEVER go home!"

Mom took me to the hospital and we went in. She taught nursing and rotated her students through that same hospital, so most everybody knew her. I signed whatever papers in good humor and entered through the glass doors that were locked behind me. My mom was my best friend, I trusted her.

I had no idea what would eventually happen. I was assigned a room and was given some medication. No one talked to me, no one examined me, just gave me dinner and another pill. The next morning, breakfast and another pill. Where was my examination? The side effect of the medicine reminded me of when I was in college and some girlfriends and I went to a music concert. They convinced me to join them in taking a Quaalude while at the concert. We had a designated driver. I never had the desire to try a "Downer" before, but they finally peer pressured me into trying one. I slept through the whole concert. They would wake me up every so often and laughed at me. All I could do was rouse up for a few seconds. I missed the whole concert. That was the last time I ever did that. At least my girlfriends took care of me because it would have been easy for any unscrupulous character to take advantage of me. The drugs the hospital gave me was a milder form, but thanks to my girlfriends, I was familiar with feeling, nonetheless. Without the staff knowing, I started flushing each pill down the toilet.

Other people were there, and each day we got together, and the group talked with a leader. I was waiting for an examination and permission to go home. About the third day, I realized the "group" consisted of; a domestic violence case; an alcoholic; two drug abusers; a rapist (we found out later); and me. WHAT DID I DO?! I went for a walk, didn't hurt anyone, didn't hurt myself, didn't cause any property damage. I didn't even threaten anyone, and drugs weren't involved! Did the unfinished painting job of kitchen cabinets make them think I was unhinged?

I hadn't yet figured out I was in the psych ward or even why I was there, but I had had enough! I walked out of the room and knew I had been locked in all this time. If I had understood the treatment, I could have signed myself out. But I didn't! The only way I could see to get out was through the nurses' window where they dispersed pills. I walked over to the nurses' window, and with my physical conditioning and agility, I jumped through the window like a cat. As I walked through to the elevator, one large guy grabbed me by the wrist.

"Get your hand OFF!" I commanded.

I didn't threaten him, I didn't ball up my fist, and when he let go, I politely smiled and said, "Thank you."

I walked right out and over to the elevators. Behind me, I could hear everybody scrambling. I waited and waited, and the elevator never came up. They were busy locking down the floor.

I picked up the phone on a nearby desk and called some friends in Kentucky.

"Come pick me up, these people here are crazy," I said.

The nurses came out and said, "We've called your mom, and she says she will come here in the morning to pick you up. Come back and wait until morning."

I looked out the window, and it was dark. I thought that made sense, I said, "Ok," and went back in. How naive could one soul be?

Taking a "walk in the wilderness" is a classic sign of depression, and my mom knew that. A broken heart did not need the treatment that was tricked on me and what was about to come.

The next morning, I was happily ready to go home. Here came my mom with several other people who I didn't know. We all went into a room and sat around a conference table. I was introduced to supposedly my lawyer, whom I had never met, a judge, hospital people and my mom. I couldn't figure out what was going on because I thought I was going home. My mom explained how I was not myself and picked up a hitchhiker, took all the handles off my grandmother's cabinets, left my friend on the side of the road and went for a walk. I'm sitting here thinking, "What's wrong helping a person in need, isn't that a Good Samaritan? Isn't that what you and my church has taught me all my life?" I took the handles off because my grandmother asked me to paint her cabinets and I will admit leaving my friend and car on the road to take a walk was a little nutty, but I didn't hurt anyone. My friend wasn't a helpless infant, and he handled the situation just fine. I think the walk just cleared my head. I sat quietly. No one asked me anything, and I was committed before I had a chance to fully process what was going on or defend my position. My appointed lawyer was utterly useless. I guessed he got paid whether he opened his mouth or not. I had never been so blindsided like this before in my life or since. I'm sure I did look confused.

Everyone left the room including me. I walked out and saw Mom.

I looked at her and said with a long, drawn-out, "Mmooooom." I couldn't believe she just did that to me.

She looked down at the ground and back at me and said, "Tell them your problems, tell them your problems."

All my life, it was a rule never to tell family problems. Why had the rules suddenly changed and what was wrong with Mom?

"Mom, I'll tell you my problem--I'm in HERE--that's my problem," I said very politely.

"No, no, tell them your problems," she said.

I was utterly flabbergasted. I had just been committed to a mental ward. Why had she forsaken me?

Almost a week went by and, **finally**, I saw someone with some authority. At the end of the hall were Mom, Dad, and the doctor, whom I had never met. I walked right up to them and began to do what she had been asking and telling what had been happening in Kentucky.

I got out about six words when the doctor quite rudely interrupted. "What day is this?" he asked.

I was put off by his rude interruption and continued with what I was saying.

He interrupted again and said, "See, she has dissociative thoughts, might be a touch bipolar. I think we will change her medicine."

I hadn't been taking medicine since the second day, so how could you change it and furthermore, I had never even seen this doctor before. He had done nothing but rudely interrupt me. How could he know anything if he has never talked to or examined me? His diagnosis was based on nothing! But one nice piece of paper of credentials on his wall and he was an expert on my life! A**hole!

My mouth fell open with dismay and I took one step backward and thought, "Oh my God! I have just entered The Twilight Zone. I have found myself in a 1950 black and white mental hospital nightmare! These people are crazy, and I'm the one locked up!"

I think my eyes blinked wide open a few times before I did an about face and walked all the way to the other end of the hall into my room.

I thought, "How in the H*LL am I going to get OUT OF HERE? And thank God I wasn't taking medicine, or I would be crazy! I needed my wits for this kind of treatment. And by the way, Dr. Know-it-all, it was THURSDAY! And besides that, who cares what day it is when YOU ARE LOCKED UP! YOU CAN'T GO ANYWHERE!"

OK, I'll play the game. When I'm supposed to sit, I'll sit. When I'm supposed to eat, I'll eat. When I'm supposed to sleep, I'll sleep. And when I'm supposed to SH**, I'LL SH**! That's what I did. After a total of twenty-eight days, I nonchalantly said to the counselor, "I'm tired of being in here, I just want to go back to work." Boom. I was out. My insurance covering mental health ran out in thirty days. I'm sure they were looking for an excuse to get rid of me.

My mom picked me up and filled the prescription that I never had and never would take. I got home and couldn't figure out what just happened to me. For a couple of days, I paced around the house thinking about what had happened and what was I going to do? "My car wouldn't start, and I didn't have a job, but that was alright, I was ready to get on with it. I was going back to work, and I was going back to Kentucky...that was the home I made for myself over the last nine years.

"Mom, I'm ready to go back to work," I said.

"Oh no, you have to wait for the medicine to kick in," she said.

So, I gave her another dose of truth, "Mom, I haven't been taking the medicine the whole time I've been home and none while I was in the hospital."

"Lisa, no one paces around the house and not be on that medicine," she said.

Again, I was dumbfounded. No matter what I said, she would not believe me. I felt like a child again with my parents having total control over everything I did.

I see why some teenagers won't talk to their parents...**what is the point of talking when no one will listen**! I don't know what she wanted to hear, and she had always taught me to tell the truth, but **every time I told the truth, I got in deeper trouble**.

I didn't figure this out until much later, but she had someone to pull the spark plug wires on my car, so I couldn't leave.

I was twenty-seven years old and I paid for everything I had in Kentucky. The little house I lived in, I paid the rent. I had bought my Toyota brand new and made the down payment and all the monthly payments. I paid for my health insurance, my landline phone, my clothes, my gas, my fun, and with all those penny ante, less than $15,000 a year jobs, I had saved close to $10,000. It was not like my mom and dad were supporting me. I was making it on my own. What had I done to deserve my life being stripped from me?!

Shortly after I got out of the hospital, she took me to see the doctor who said I might be a touch bipolar. I went into his office and sat in front of his desk. I didn't know why I was there; I thought he was an a**hole anyway.

"What makes bums?" I asked.

"What kind of bums?" he asked.

"People that don't work," I said. That's what I felt like because I wasn't working and that was all I wanted to do, go back to work.

"Well some bums become street people, and they are schizophrenic. You might have a touch of that," he said.

What an a**hole and a credentialled a**hole to boot. I didn't want to hear Dr. Know-It-All anymore, so I just sat. When I went out to the car where my mom was waiting, I told her what he had said. She locked her jaw, put the car in drive and I never had to go back to him again.

Years later, my husband was talking about intervening on a psychiatrist at the hospital, and mom recognized he was the doctor over my care. When doctors get caught drugging, they must go to a drug program or lose their license. Tom was on that intervention group for him.

"He was CCCRRAAAZZYYY. He came from the most f***ed up dysfunctional family I have ever heard, and I've heard a lot! He was abusing an unbelievable amount of prescription drugs," Tom said.

Mom said, if she would have known that, she would have sued him for malpractice. Too bad it was many years later. H*ll, I knew he was crazy! But who listened to me!

When I went outside, Mom went with me. I couldn't drive anywhere because my car was rigged. I was afraid to pack up and leave, I was afraid she would call the cops to pick me up, and I would be committed again. I was trapped in my childhood home. She had me sign power of attorney and took over my bank account and paid my bills. I didn't know what I was supposed to do because I had already done everything she wanted. I'm sure she thought she was helping.

I was so bored watching daytime soap operas. I just got slower and slower. Finally, I didn't see the point getting out of bed. There was nothing to do and no way to get out. I even got tired of talking because no one ever really heard what I said. She took me to another charter hospital I didn't want to go to and spent all my hard-earned money on my treatment. I just wanted to go back to work and get on with my life.

When I got into that hospital, I just went to bed.

Oh, my God, how the nurses would harp on me. "Llliissaa, we know you can get out of bed because it's not wet."

I thought, "Who said I couldn't get out of bed; I just don't see the point." But, I got tired of them harping on me. I played the same game as before.

I think my stay lasted about three weeks. I had acquired the hospital records about ten years later because I needed them to get health insurance. I read the doctor was beginning to suspect my mom was over controlling. Ya think? When I got out, she took me to that doctor on an outpatient basis. I was reluctant to talk because I had learned my lesson about telling the truth and I always knew lies got you in trouble. I did tell my new doctor many times I was trapped. I don't think she ever understood I wasn't trapped in my head; I was caught in reality! I did tell her once that I didn't think my dad ever loved me and she replied, "This is good stuff!" I didn't understand how that was "good stuff" and went back to not talking. Now I understand she was glad I was opening up.

The "wear down" tactic from every direction had taken its toll. I was so confused from all the so-called "treatment," the original problem of a broken heart became buried for years to come.

Mom took me to the State Mental Hospital to get Social Security disability benefits for me because all my money was gone. I said, "No," and she made me go anyway. I sat there and never took my eyes off the floor. I can't express how demeaning the whole experience was. Why did I need government support? I was perfectly capable of supporting myself. Thank God the doctor told her it was a treatable condition and I didn't qualify. If Disability had been approved for me and the money never ran out, I might not have ever escaped. I felt like I had been in the armpit of the world. Growing up, we would tease each other about going to the Mental Hospital. It was nowhere we wanted to go. Only scum went there. It was the stigma many people had of mental illness.

I got out of the charter hospital and nothing changed. I was still trapped. I wanted this nightmare to stop, and I started to think about a bullet through the head or a razor blade across the wrist. I was moving so slowly that I could imagine the bullet taking minutes to get across my brain and what if I missed and was in a vegetative state. Well, this situation did suck, but it could be worse. I couldn't figure out a quick enough way to die, so I gave up suicide as a solution.

Finally, my mom informed me she and my doctor had decided shock treatment was the only option, but I had to sign for it. I said, "No." Every day she came in, and every day I said, "No." After a while, she committed me yet again. Still, I wouldn't sign. Every day, she came in. Now, I FINALLY got ugly.

"NO Mom, I said NO!" Same thing, every day. "NO, Mom, GET THE F*** AWAY FROM ME!" She still wouldn't quit. I don't think I had ever said the f-word in front of my mother or even to that day, let alone AT her. But the nagging was more than I could take.

The end of my rope was unusually long, but FINALLY, I got so d*mn fed up with her, I finally gave in.

"Ok Mom, I'll make a deal with you. I--WILL HAVE SHOCK TREATMENT--IF YOU WILL AGREE--TO LEAVE ME--THE F*** ALONE! -- IS THAT A DEAL MOM?!"

"Oh, yes, oh, yes," she said.

"THAT'S NOT GOOD ENOUGH--YOU WRITE ME A CONTRACT--THAT YOU WILL LEAVE ME--THE F*** ALONE-- AND I WILL HAVE F***ING SHOCK TREATMENT! YOU GOT THAT! AND F***ING SIGN IT! -- RIGHT F***ING NOW!!!" I demanded!

And FINALLY, she left me alone!

I can laugh now and tell you she scrambled for a piece of paper out of her pocketbook and that contract, I kept for years, was on the back of a small grocery receipt. But it was signed!

Not only did she leave me alone, everybody left me alone. I didn't have to go to those stupid group sessions. I didn't have to eat if I didn't want. I didn't have to do a damn thing that I didn't want. And I never had to speak to another living soul! Thank God, they let me live in PEACE! Once a week, they wheeled me down for shock treatment. It was like surgery. They knocked me out with a drug, and later I woke up. I rarely ever slept, and at least I was glad to have a break from my reality!

This hospital unit was a little more comfortable than the others, with a living room and a comfy couch. I stretched out with my feet up and watched some TV. I rolled a wheelchair to the end of the hall and sat for hours in a sunbeam. Occasionally, I would move the chair to stay in the sunbeam. I peered into the rubber room and wondered when they would decide I needed to be in there. Luckily, I never had that experience.

A girl about my age started to come in everyday, early afternoon, and talk to me for about an hour. I was usually on the couch, and I never spoke and rarely looked her direction. She talked and talked and talked about her boyfriend, her family, and whatever else came to her mind. Then she would leave. Every day it was the same thing.

Finally, one day she said, "You're my best friend." I thought, "Oh God, that was sad. I had yet ever to say a word."

One day, she talked me into going into the art room equipped with lots of drawing supplies. I sat across the table and watched her doodle and doodle and doodle, while she talked and talked and talked. I finally got tired of watching her scratch around on paper. I pulled out a piece of paper and drew her portrait, then handed it to her. She was ecstatic and went out and showed anyone who would look. I heard a lot of chatter. I got up, walked out and went back to the couch. The next day, it was the same thing. In the past, I struggled with doing artwork because it was never perfect enough. This lock-up was quite a freeing art experience because now, I didn't care.

All the nurses wanted portraits. I began to get amused at watching them ask, but my expression never changed. They would come in and stand ten to fifteen feet away not to bother me and very, very politely say, "I don't want to bother you, but will you draw my portrait?"

I would nod, and they would leave. I only sketched the nurses' portraits when the spirit moved me. That was entertaining in itself. When I was ready, I was entirely indifferent to what was going on around them.

The nurses' station was a flurry of activity. I walked up to the counter in slow motion and softly said, "I'm ready." The world stopped! They would cut their phone calls short, shut the files that were open, quit whatever they were doing and sail in to sit for a portrait! It wasn't museum quality, just a colored pastel sketch, dead on their likeness, and they were overwhelmingly pleased. I don't know if they were pleased because they got a portrait or because I finally showed some life. But they were energized. They compared each other's pictures. All my artwork was hanging on the wall behind the nurses' station.

I often wondered if the girl who came to visit was a patient or a counselor. She dressed like a patient. Only once I went to look for her and I didn't see her, but I didn't put much effort into looking. Didn't matter, I knew she would be back the next day. Her visits were pleasant.

I had been there about four weeks. My doctor came in and said, "Wow, who's doing these?" as she admired the portraits on the wall. Without a word, they pointed twice, like pushing a button, in my direction. She looked at those portraits, looked at me, looked back at the pictures, and scratched on her clipboard. That was the end of shock treatment. It was only three, the minimum, she said.

The shock treatment affected my short-term memory. One obvious result was the treatment made it hard to think of the right word in the middle of a conversation. It took **years** to get over that result. Since I think "in pictures," I could make a snapshot of a scene to picture in my mind to refer to later. It screwed my photographic memory. Maybe if I concentrated on it enough, I might develop it again. I've gotten along fine without it.

I hope the practice of shock treatment has ended. It was useless and damaging to me. I look at mental illness entirely differently. Is it the people who are committed that have a problem, or the people around them who are the problem? There is a big difference in forcing mental illness as a solution to a person's problem as opposed to someone voluntarily seeking mental health.

The peace, the girlfriend, the understanding of nurses and being appreciated for my work were the solution to my mistreatment. It is merely that kindness heals. Most importantly, it doesn't take a doctor to prescribe kindness. Anyone can do it, even animals, especially a Saddle Horse. Kindness had great power.

No one gave me a way out, I earned my way "out of the box" by using my art talent. I was driven home to my childhood home and everyday my mom and I walked down the road and around the corner to the barn and riding ring my dad had built for us when I was a teenager. I felt like I was on a leash. I would groom and ride my horse and then we would walk back. It became my routine.

Around this time, my nephew was born. Mom, with great excitement took me to see him and my sister-in-law in the hospital. I didn't want to go. I looked at that innocent, helpless infant and thought, "Are these people crazy? Why on earth would anyone want to bring a child into this world of a living h*ll?" I never said a word.

My legs had been cut out from under me and I couldn't figure out what was wrong with me. I think I was too afraid to go back to where I had made my home. I had to start over whether I wanted to or not, so I started over with what I had in front of me and what I had learned.

People commissioned portraits or artwork of something. I rented a house next door from my grandmother and set up an art studio. Once, I painted sixteen hours straight, slept two and painted seven more hours, detailing a design on furniture to help the local furniture factory make deadline for market. I designed logos, church cookbooks, sold photographs, constructed and painted signs. I did pencil drawings, pastels, oils, whatever opportunity that came up. My girlfriends and I put together an art show with the choice artwork and in one afternoon, I had work for two more years. I funded my horse business with the modest proceeds. After all day at the studio, I built fences and stalls until eleven o'clock at night. I had endless energy fueled by resentment from losing my freedom and assets. Shock treatment was very successful at burying my issues for years to come. The hardness of oak fence boards and locust posts was no match for me. I could drive a nail like a freight train. Everything I loved in Kentucky was gone. No house, no money, no nothing.

So, by God, I'll build a little piece of Kentucky as my own. I HAD a dream and I was determined to LIVE IT one way or another.

In time, I traveled back to Kentucky to Lexington Junior League Horse Show and to the World Championship in Louisville. Prince Charming phoned me and asked if I remembered him loaning me $100.

"Could you pay me back? I'll meet you at the Lexington Horse Show," he suggested. I agreed. I met him alone in the middle of a crowd and handed him a $100 bill. All he wanted to talk about was his infant daughter and how hard it was for him to hold her while the doctor gave her childhood shots. All I could think about was, "That should have been MY daughter." How could I respond to that? I never said a word.

I said a polite goodbye and went back to Virginia.

After years and years and years, Mark was the best of my Kentucky dream.

Now, he's gone.

V

Finding My Footing

After the Breakthrough

Now, the situation with the church took on a new, distasteful flavor. I knew first-hand what it was like to be teamed up against and that was precisely what they were unknowingly doing. I saw my childhood friend again at the Wellness Center and informed him that I was trying to get through to the church to change the sign. I jokingly told him they all thought I was crazy and since he was the judge, would he please not sign the order when they decided to have me committed.

"You are the only sane one over there," he said, very nonchalantly.

I was relieved with his comment. It was a calming conversation to have someone in power hear and support me. Had it been the sixteenth century, I would have been burned at the stake as a witch because I thought differently. In this century, I was committed to a mental hospital because I thought differently. I don't think God intended us to think alike. If so, where would creativity come from? Or should that word be creation?

I texted the preacher and invited him to the barn for coffee. He had visited the barn many times, but now he would only meet with me if my husband was there. My husband didn't want to be bothered. Every time I asked the preacher to talk out our differences, he always had to have someone there on his side. I've experienced being teamed up on before. No way. He texted me to stop talking to other members and stop working on the website. Who died and left him King? Or should I say, God?

I received an official letter from the preacher and the Clerk of the Session concerning the website and sign. It informed me I would be paid $250 for the domain name, hosting and website design and all were to be turned over to the church. If I chose not to take the money I was to take down the site and not to work on it anymore.

I had every right to keep control of the website because it was my work. I was planning to give the website to the church after finishing it, and everyone had their input. But after the way I was treated, if they wanted to buy it, they could pay me what it was worth. Thirty years ago, my time was billed out at $30 to $50 an hour. I had to call Kentucky to ask the market price of my design time. It had more than doubled. $250 was a drop in the bucket and barely covered my expenses. But the only option was his way or the highway. I sent the money back with a polite note and wished them well on their new website.

Why did the preacher have to have control over my work? Why did the agent, buyer, and vet have to have control over my horse? Why did my mom have to have control over my life? What is it with people who must have control? Can't they just control themselves?

The next part of the preacher's letter was the roadmap for putting a sign proposal to the church session. By a specific date, I needed to have a written proposal, or the option was closed. If fulfilled by a particular time, my presentation would be accepted, and I had the first twenty minutes in the meeting. There were a lot of hoops in which to jump, but it was important to me to support my childhood friend. The Golden Rule says, "Do unto others as you would have them do unto you." I would have liked a someone to stand up for me. Besides, it was my Granddaddy's church I wanted to help with my talent. I worked extremely hard on this proposal. I had no idea if it would change their minds, but I thought it was the right thing to do.

On another front, I called my mom and asked her if my husband and I could speak with her and my stepdad together to let me explain what went on with the preacher and me. This time, I wasn't going to sit silently without defending myself as I did twenty-five years ago.

Mom suggested to come over after church on Sunday. I agreed. I had the letters and texts between the preacher and me, which proved how polite I was and how dictating he was. My professional sign proposal was completed. It was all in black and white to prove to her that "I didn't need a doctor or a grief counselor."

I stayed away from the church since this whole blowup happened. I couldn't believe how I had been treated. Not one person out of the entire church called me for condolences when I lost my horse, which was everything I had worked for. I received one church card, it lifted one brick. The preacher had told me he looked at the church as a place of healing. Healing for whom?

I felt as though they were accusing all the wrongs on me. No matter who was wrong, I was blamed. I kept telling my husband, "They are crucifying me, they are crucifying me."

During this time, a very odd thing happened: a spot of poison ivy rash appeared on the bottom of my left foot while I was walking around Hillsville Labor Day Flea Market. The place was a perfect circle. A few days later, I was sitting in my recliner with my feet up, my right foot on top of my left. I glanced down and saw a stream of dried blood that ran from the middle of my right foot to the end of my second toe. It reminded me of Jesus's feet in the crucifix picture. My eyes became as big as saucers because I already knew there was a spot in the bottom of the left foot. What if there was a spot on my palms? I squinted when checking my fate. Fearfully and slowly I turned my hand over. It was clean! Whew, what a relief! I laughed.

I decided now wasn't the time to deal with my mom. I wasn't ready. My husband and I decided it was a great idea to wait. I would take her the paperwork to read and go swimming instead.

Before I could pick up the phone and tell her my plan, the phone rang.

"Well I'm at Walmart buying your lunch, and we'll be over shortly," Mom said.

"At Walmart? No Mom. I was coming over there!" I stammered.

"Well I told Tom we were coming," she said.

My heart began to race!

"No Mom. Today is not a good day," I said.

"Well, you said, you said..." she insisted.

"Ooohkaaay," I said as I decided to let the chips fall and we hung up.

"You didn't tell me she was coming over here!" I excitedly said to Tom.

"I didn't know," he said and looked surprise.

I threw my hands up in the air. "I'm not sitting at the table with her. I'm walking across the pasture to check my apples on the tree, sit and try to relax. When y'all are finished eating, call me, and I'll walk back and be calm by then," I said.

Tom liked and agreed to my plan.

It was time to face the music and I invited them into the living room to talk, my mom, my stepdad, my husband and me. I calmly started talking about what had happened and read the texts between the preacher and me. When I read his poor choice of words, she bristled up on the edge of the couch, gave me the nastiest look, and I knew what it meant. "How dare I say anything that would make THE PREACHER LOOK BAD!" I started to defend myself. Even my stepdad added, "Well, it wasn't very pastoral." I liked the fact my new stepdad supported me. But my mom wouldn't back down and insisted I was the one in the wrong. It made me so mad, I was spitting my words!

"You, you, you need anger management!" she responded.

"NO" doesn't work with her, so I said, "Well, if I need anger management, so does my brother."

My husband popped up and agreed. We are not often on the same page, but he knew if that were the criteria, I wouldn't have to go. She would never send the Golden Boy, the doctor, to anger management.

She would not hear a word I said and she and my stepdad, who is a retired doctor, thought I needed to be on medication.

That was it! I put my foot down! "I'LL tell you what I NEED--I need you, my brother, sister-in-law, and the preacher--TO STAY AWAY FROM ME! I demanded.

"Well!" she said and left.

My husband and I could not believe what we just saw.

But, oh, praise God, I was free! I just cut a couple more ties that bind, Mom and the church. No one was taking control over me again. YES! Once I got past the grief of my horse, I had found my God, or myself, as God dwells within me. How quickly everyone was forcing their will on me. Why did everyone want control over me? All I wanted was to help my childhood friend with my God-given talent and help the church too. What was wrong with that idea? I'm not forcing my will on anyone. I have always been perfectly capable of controlling myself, and I haven't hurt anyone in the process. I have always tried to go by their rules, but this time, they can live by my rules.

In a few days, my mom called my husband.

"We have to do something about Lisa. Her stepdad thinks she should be on medication," she said.

"There's nothing wrong with her, and she gets like this. She's my wife, and I'm sticking by her," he said. My husband stepped up and gave me the best support of our entire marriage. That was the most fabulous luxury he had ever provided me!

Mom later called, and chit chatted with my girlfriend.

"Her stepdad thinks Lisa should be on medication," she finally came to her point.

"She'll be alright," my girlfriend said. Now, my friends are standing up for me! Thank you, God, for the support!

I was bouncing like a ball between being high and happy to low and hurt. But I was free! When I was high and happy, my creativity was off the chart. I took my husband and my friend on the rollercoaster ride with me. They never knew what to expect from me.

Breaking out of the box, I had many ideas flying around in my head. At one point, I was talking a mile a minute, waving my arms about while marching back and forth in front of the fireplace. My husband was sitting on the couch as a captive audience, and his head was following me like he was watching a ping pong match. I finally stopped and shut up.

"Ummm. Is this the creative process?" he asked.

"THIS....IS IT!" I said in a high pitch voice. My arms flew up like the end of a command performance. I never had creativity like this! This abundance was awesome!

We laughed about it for days. It was the greatest natural high I think I ever had! But that wasn't all. I did the most original monologues, I'm sorry we didn't videotape them because I don't have a clue how they went, but the comedy content was hilarious. I was amusing my husband, and I decided to include him in the act while we were standing in the kitchen.

"Ok...I'll be Gladys Knight, and you be the Pip. Do this and say, "Walk this way. Talk this way." I showed him how to mechanically move his arms and hands and walk like a robot.

I started into the monolog, and my husband broke into character with robot movements, chanting "Walk this way, talk this way." After listening to my shenanigans for about thirty seconds, he broke down in laughter. With the interruption, a look of shock came across my face. Abruptly, my monolog stopped. I marched up to him.

"YOU ARE NOT HARVEY KORMAN, because I know I'M NOT TIM CONWAY!" I announced. My husband hit the floor in uncontrollable laughter, and I could no longer keep a straight face. "See... I told you I wasn't Tim Conway." He could always keep a straight face. My husband was laughing so hard while holding his stomach as he rolled back and forth on the floor.

I seized the chance to include my friend in our fun, and on her birthday, we took her out of town to a unique hideaway to dinner. She and my husband sat in the front of her SUV, while I slept in the back seat. The bouncing ball of emotion wore me out. Every feeling I had was intense, and I wondered if they could feel it too. I got out of the car with a warm sense of love. I gave my husband a big hug. As we walked toward the restaurant, I gave my friend a big birthday hug. When we crossed the road, I looked around and my husband and my best friend were hugging in the middle of the street! Anybody seeing us had to wonder what was going on with those people. We laughed and laughed!

We sat near the front at an old wooden table in the quaint little restaurant, renovated from an old hardware store. After the waiter took our order, my husband and I thought we would share our comedy act with my friend. First came the monologue... then my husband started his robot rhythm... "walk this way, talk this way"...then my friend, the free spirit she is, joined in, "do wop, do wop," making silly hand motions side to side, in unison with the robot. None of us could take the comedy routine for very long, and we broke into loud laughter.

Soon, my husband excused himself to the restroom, which was past a solid staircase and to the left. I looked over at my friend and said, "I'll bet you $100 that he 'walks this way and talks this way' when he reappears from behind the staircase."

Grinning, we stared in the direction of the staircase with great anticipation. My husband reappeared and instantly fell into character with his robot movements. We broke down into loud laughter for the second time. I would think everyone in the restaurant had to wonder what we were having. As we left, I apologized to the hostess if our laughter was too loud and disturbed their other guests.

"Oh no, we love it when our guests are having fun. Pleeeease come back anytime," she begged. With an ear to ear grin, I thanked her.

The next day, I thought about my mother and her protection of the preacher. It's not hard to understand when I tell you my beloved Granddaddy, a preacher, was her father. Apparently, above all else, protect the preacher. Real men of God are worth protecting.

That is a story all in itself.

16

My Granddaddy Query

Granddaddy was truly a man of God. He was kind and gentle, and he devoted his life to serving God and others. I loved to sit and talk with him, and he was glad to do so. When I was most interested in sitting and talking, he was retired and had the time to spend with me.

He was born on December 18, 1897, as one of ten children, five boys, and five girls, growing up on a farm near Concord, North Carolina. Times were hard, and everyone in the family had to work. He shared about bringing his earnings to the table when he was eleven, and his mother would take his ten or eleven pennies and give him one or two back. He spoke about when he heard the call into the service of ministry at fifteen years old. His mother, father, and minister helped to map his plan. Just as he started on the program at Davidson College in North Carolina, WWI broke out. He felt called to serve in the army. The Army turned him down because of a handicap he had from birth, his right arm was out of the socket at his shoulder, an easy fix with today's orthopedics. He was determined to serve and accomplished enlisting.

Granddaddy was sent to France and put in charge of a horse-drawn cannon brigade at the rank of corporal in Battery "F" of the 113th Field Artillery. His enlistment record shows he was involved in several battles and skirmishes and his character as excellent. No AWOL or absences.

When he returned home, he finished school, and a single, sweet school teacher caught his eye. Mary Estelle Luck was my grandmother's name, and she was born in 1902 in Bedford County,

Virginia, the only girl among six brothers. She told me many stories about her childhood family and one I liked best was about her father riding his horse from Bedford, Virginia, to Louisville, Kentucky, to attend the seminary to study to become a Baptist minister. He passed through the Cumberland Gap, which touches four states, Virginia, West Virginia, Tennessee, and Kentucky on his ten-day ride. There were wonderful love letters, my cousin informed me, written between my great-grandmother and him. Without phones and emails, the anticipation of a love letter must have been incredible.

Grandma used to say how handsome her father was on his dapple-gray horse. I thought that was a fascinating comment until I inherited a rather large, framed picture of him. When I saw the picture of my great-grandfather, I understood her admiration. It pictured a very distinguished man with salt and pepper colored hair and a salt and pepper mustache. I bet he did look handsome on his dapple-gray horse. She loved her daddy; most little girls do.

My grandmother attended James Madison College to become a school teacher. She held the position in Montvale, Virginia, when Granddaddy was the preacher at the Montvale Presbyterian Church. At the same time, he also served several outlying churches. They met when both lived in the hotel as two young people starting out. In time, they were married and moved to the house provided by the church. A wealthy lady who lived in the same hotel gave her silverware set to my grandmother as a wedding gift. It was one of my grandmother's most cherished possessions.

I remember as a small child sitting with her in big, cushy chair while she worked the newspaper's crossword puzzle. It was my job to draw the letter in the appropriate square. I didn't even know my alphabet as she patiently drew the letters with her finger on her thigh. When she almost finished the letter, I would say, "Oh, I know, I know, Grandma." I was so smart.

Her repeating lessons over the years were, "Family is the most important. You must learn to be patient and you must learn to be gracious." Lessons for a southern lady. I was named after my grandmother, Mary Estelle. Mary Lisa was the name I was given by my mother. Other members of the family knew Grandma as Aunt Tell. Maybe it was her job to hand down stories about the family, rules and Southern traditions. There were lots of "this is how this is done." Her fried chicken was to die for.

She was with Granddaddy when he attended the funeral of his last remaining brother. As he drove away his comment was, "Well, that's a closed chapter." People don't live forever, he made the most of the time he had until it was gone.

My grandparents never really had very much because wherever Granddaddy felt he was called to serve a congregation, the church always provided them with a house known as the church manse. They had one car and some furniture. I don't think they wanted for more. Their motto was, "Waste not, want not." The picture of them together always seemed to be such a perfect fit and yet, Granddaddy was 5'9," and Grandma was 4'11."

My grandparents left Montvale when he heard the call, as he would say, to Mossy Creek, Virginia. WWII broke out, and he again felt called to serve. The army told him he was too old. He accomplished his enlistment and served as a chaplain. This time, he entered with the rank of Captain as he had completed seven years of college earning an A.B. and B.D. in Theology and five weeks Chaplain School in Harvard, Massachusetts. He was not supposed to go overseas and yet the Army sent him to England. I always heard he and several chaplains made the cover of Time-Life Magazine sometime during wartime. There must be a copy somewhere.

My uncle gave me a copy of Granddaddy's discharge papers from both World Wars. On the bottom of the Separation Qualification Record on 16 April 1946 was the Summary of Military Occupations:

CHAPLAIN: Conducted Religious Services. Ministered to the sick, wounded and imprisoned. Corresponded with relatives of the ill, deceased, and troubled personnel. Delivered lectures on sexual morality and orientation. Cooperated with Special Services Officers, American Red Cross and Community Organizations in stimulating the morals, entertainment and research work. Conferred with Commanding Officers on religious and patriotic observance and questions of morals and morale.

AUTHORIZED: The European Theatre of Operation Ribbon. The World War II Victory Medal. The World War I Army of Occupation Ribbon and the World War I Victory Ribbon.

While he was in the army, my grandmother went back to her hometown of Bedford, Virginia, where she taught school, and by then she had two children, my mom, and uncle.

Granddaddy survived both World Wars without a scratch, but I don't know how anyone survives the war without at least emotional scars. If he did, I never saw them. After the war, he loaded up his family and went to Hillsville. He served as minister to the Hillsville Presbyterian Church plus several outlying churches, Fairview, Gilman, Webb. Grandma always took part in teaching Sunday school, Vacation Bible School, and women's circles.

When he arrived in Hillsville, the church building was a wooden one-room structure with a single coal burning stove and no bathrooms. Today, the old building houses a used furniture and antique store. The original church building was in the middle of town across from the old Courthouse and was destroyed by fire along with several other buildings in 1890.

In 1946 upon Granddaddy's arrival, he saw the need for a new church building. He assembled several of the respected men and women of the community, and with his leadership, they secured the site and land, raised money, traveled to see other possible church floor plans, worked with the architect, hired the contractors and finished the current building in 1952.

One day while checking on the construction, he heard a voice calling for help. A curious young man had fallen down the chimney, and Granddaddy had the fire department rescue him. He did whatever was necessary to care for people. He was a faithful missionary to many underserved communities.

In 1957, he heard the calling again, left and went to New Monmouth Presbyterian Church near Lexington, Virginia. Not everyone can say that they were baptized by their grandfather, a veteran of two World Wars, but my brothers and I can. It was there in Lexington I was baptized. I like this spot because it is not far from the Virginia Horse Center. He and my grandmother later retired in Bedford, Virginia, to her childhood home place, built around 1907.

We all loved to go "over the hills and through the woods to Grandmother's house we go." The trip was two hours away, and we always went on Thanksgiving. They came to celebrate Christmas and Easter, and we made excuses to go there. My grandmother always served us with her cherished silverware and her fried chicken. I liked going a week in the summer where I slept to eleven o'clock on a real feather mattress on an antique wrought iron bed. It felt more like a nest than a bed, and I slept like a rock.

By today's standards, there was nothing to do, only three TV stations, no internet, no cell phones, no video games. The pillowed porch swing provided many hours of entertainment. Sometimes Granddaddy and I would pitch a twelve-inch green speckled plastic ball as I would swing. The big wooden banister was a slide from upstairs to downstairs with a well-positioned pillow padding the big wooden ball on top of the post at the end. My grandmother was more concerned for my bottom than her house.

The driveway was a beautiful gravel lane over a quarter mile long, and at fourteen, Granddaddy taught me to drive his metallic dark green Dodge Dart as we drove to the mailbox and back. We would shoot his 22 rifle, and I was required to draw a target on a piece of cardboard, complete with a colored-in bullseye and enlarging circles. The process of making the artwork helped to pass the time. We took turns, shot, put the gun down, walked to the target, inspected where we had hit the mark, circled it with a magic marker and walked back. Did it again. A lesson in patience and accuracy. My brothers got the same lesson. We didn't need an assault rifle to hit our target, only one bullet. Barney Fife only had one.

There was a rope swing in the backyard with a wooden board with a notch on each end to position the rope. When finished swinging, the wooden seat was put in out of the weather, not to waste a board from water damage. "Waste not, want not" was one of Granddaddy's mottos. The swing was hanging from a limb of more than a one-hundred-year-old walnut tree Great Granddaddy Luck had planted. I swung for hours and watched the clouds make patterns. My grandparents grew a lot of their vegetables and complained of a pesky rabbit eating their plants. I spent hours trying to catch him with a carrot and a box propped up on a stick with a string tied to it. I never trapped the rabbit, but it wasn't because I didn't try.

There was a one-room schoolhouse in the backyard too. It contained a daybed, an old piano where I played chopsticks and various simple silly tunes, a bookshelf which I have, various garden and yard tools. When all the cousins got together, we used the same green speckled plastic ball and played a game called "Annie Over." We would split up evenly and get on opposite sides of the schoolhouse. One side would have the ball and announce "Annie," and the other side would answer "Over." The first side threw the ball over the schoolhouse and ran to the other side. The object was to get to the other side before someone caught the ball and hit you with it. If hit by the ball, you were out. We would line up again on each side and keep playing. The last person left won. Most of the time the adults couldn't resist playing with us. The game was simple, and the fun was great!

A Concord grapevine, no telling how old, grew on a trellis in the front yard. Every September, we would go for "the jelly making." We teased Granddaddy about his grape juice that accidentally fermented into wine. "The PREACHER is not SUPPOSED to make WINE, we teased!" He got a big kick out of the attention.

And speaking of attention, he operated with the discipline of a soldier. He was up every day at six am, ate lunch exactly at noon, except on Sunday, took a nap at one o'clock, had supper precisely at six pm and to bed at eleven. His clothes were always hung up or folded, and he kept his socks and underwear neatly folded in the drawer. He always helped with the dishes, and his job was to dry and put them in the cabinets. The trash was tidy, and he burned what he could in the incinerator, he called it, which was a metal 55-gallon drum with a hole cut at the bottom on one side for air.

The garage was not connected to the house but about seventy-five feet away. It was kept neat along with the car, lawn mower and anything they had. The Yahtzee game had rubber bands around the scorecards, and we all liked to play it, sitting around the dining room table. My mom laughs at the time we were playing when I was small, and apparently, I wasn't winning. The person who won the game rubbed in their win with laughter. I thought a new rule needed implementing. "Let's not laugh when we win." I guess I thought we should have more sportsmanlike conduct. I can promise that rule never happened. It just created more laughter.

One thing I would never forget was walking with Granddaddy. We would walk to the top of the hill and into the cool of the woods. I'm only 5'4" now and even smaller at the time, and I always remember looking way up to him, I guess in more ways than one. He always had a walking stick, and his gait was like a very slow march. Maybe that came from moving across France during the war, perhaps it was just age, or maybe it was so my little legs could keep up. But every time I wanted to talk to him, he stopped, propped both hands on his walking stick and gave me his undivided attention. I felt so important. Just to be listened to as a small child like I was the only person in the world. I never knew him listening to me would be such a touching and lasting memory. It makes me cry to think about it. I have his walking stick as one of my most prized possessions. As soon as it was mine, I carved THY ROD AND THY STAFF on it, because it reminded me of him.

His walking stick was leaning in the corner of my kitchen for years and years, rarely noticed, but I always knew it was there. One day it was gone. My husband can tell you: "Hell hath no fury like a missing walking stick." He was cleaning up and put it in a closet outside. My prized possession regained its place in record time.

Watching Granddaddy walk with his walking stick was a picture which has stuck in my mind, and I hope to carry that unique vision with me for the rest of my life. It had a reverence feel to it. Rev. S. M. Query, Sr. was usually how his name was listed, S.M. stood for Stafford Morrison. He was mentioned in the book "The Man Who Moved a Mountain," the Bob Childress story, with Granddaddy's name misprinted as Sam. He and Bob were great friends. Bob's mission was to bring peace to the area of Buffalo Mountain when there was nothing to do but make moonshine liquor, drink, carry guns and sometimes shoot each other. Are frontier times on the way back?

During Granddaddy's retirement in Bedford, people from miles away would come to sit in the rocking chairs on the front porch and drink iced tea with him to ask for his wisdom. Truly, he was a man of God. I know what it is like to see a man walk with God, a very rare vision in today's world. I want to spend the rest of my life in a walk with God, not running the race. I've already been there, done that.

It was getting near the end of his life, and I sat down with him at the dining room table while my grandmother was sitting across the room in a chair, peddling on an apparatus clamped to her wooden chair for exercise. I asked him to tell me a story of his life like I asked many times before. This time, he told of a new story. He said while in WWI, he had gotten lost from his battalion. He was walking around in the countryside of France lost when he came upon a farmhouse, and how nice the people were to take him in temporarily. He delighted at what a beautiful teenage daughter they had. He went from England to France at the end of his duty in the WWII to search out the same farmhouse. The daughter was now a grown woman with a child the right age between the years of the wars. I asked him if the child was his. He said no. I believed him. Having integrity was a fundamental trait of my family. He was an excellent example. Of all the things, he could tell me, what was the point of the farm girl story? Will I ever know?

I think you can understand how Mom could protect the preacher. She just got a little confused with which preacher she was defending. In her defense, one thing in this life I know to be true; no one is perfect.

17

Getting Away

I felt the strongest calling to finish what I had started concerning the sign presentation. I had a question with the process and called the Clerk of Session as the church letter suggested. She was a lovely lady. She answered the phone, and I identified myself.

"I'm not supposed to be talking to you," she replied.

"That's not what it said in the letter you signed," I said. I was surprised by her response.

"I didn't write the letter, I was told to sign it," she responded.

I couldn't believe what I just heard. The Session position was the same as being a Board member, and she has no power? What's with that?

"Ok, thanks for your time and I'm sorry to bother you," I said.

I was trying to play by the rules, but the rules kept changing. It was almost like I had entered into man's favorite game of football where his strategy was putting up as many blockers as possible.

I realized how uncomfortable the whole situation had become and I had asked another Session member, who I greatly respected, to read my presentation at the meeting. I thought it would make everyone involved more comfortable if I was not there. In the letter from the church, it addressed this, and the Session would only allow the presentation if I presented myself. I was informed again I had to go by this rule. It was confusing to know which rules applied and which did not.

I put my presentation in before the deadline and decided to take a trip to see some horse friends to whom I owed a thank you and to get "out of Dodge." Maybe things would cool down before my presentation in a couple of weeks.

I loaded up my car to be away for a few days, and I felt free to be driving through the beautiful countryside in Virginia to Tennessee. I couldn't remember the last time I took a trip for my enjoyment. I had my music selections and was alone with my thoughts. Since I was going to end up in Kentucky, I thought about the last time I had been to the Tattersall Saddlebred Sales located at The Red Mile in Lexington. It had been thirteen years. The sale site had been sold, torn down, and replaced with hotels. Why had I been away for so long, when I loved Kentucky so?

It wasn't hard for me to answer that question. I had been living under my husband's dysfunction of my marriage. He was a product of a household with an alcoholic father and he had his own addictions. We had some good times, but most of the time was incredibly stressful. There was a twenty-two-year difference in our ages. His two adult children lived elsewhere, and I never dreamed they would be a problem. Their mother died of colon cancer when they were in their twenties. The daughter has done quite well but, his adult son has struggled with serious drug abuse problems. I had little idea of the problem I would have to deal with it after I married.

I tried to stay out of the prior family problems until one day his adult son walked up to me and said, "Do you realize Dad is doing the same thing to your son as he did to me?" He validated what I had been thinking.

At that point I had two choices: I could either leave and take my son with me, or I could stay and help solve both problems. I was afraid my son might later resent that I had taken him from his father. I chose to stay.

Down deep, my husband is a very kind, caring and giving person. That is the person most people see. But there was chaos in our household. Was it a wife's duty to keep up appearances?

No one really knows what goes on in marriages. I can honestly say that living with problems that stem from drug and alcohol abuse is best described as a living hell for all involved.

I tried my best to get my husband to deal with his codependent son a different way. I never called my husband names or verbally abused him, but he couldn't say the same towards me. I found the bathtub to be my solace where I could be comforted for hours in the evening and to soak in peace. Every day I sought peace for a short while.

While driving through Tennessee, I thought back on the chaos. The adult son was an unbelievably talented musician who had turned to drugs. I felt he had been beaten down from the results of drug and alcohol abuse from his recovering father, my husband. The son and father shared the same dysfunction because my husband's father was also an alcoholic. Dysfunction was passed down from generation to generation until someone stopped it. I wasn't used to chaos. My mother ran a very organized and structured environment. I couldn't understand why they didn't just stop the craziness. Unfortunately for me, that became my job, to stop it before it infected my son.

My husband and I got along great in the beginning. He was a pathologist, a laboratory doctor who diagnoses health problems by viewing tissue samples under a microscope. His expertise to tell a surgeon the extent of a problem may result in a patient losing a part or all of an organ. Some organs people cannot live without, so the problem may not be surgically removed and possibly chemo treatment will help. His job could be stressful and rightly so.

His first wife was diagnosed with colon cancer when his children were in their early twenties. One doctor wanted to do chemo, and the couple decided not to accept the treatment. It would only make his wife's life worse for what remaining time she had. The family was mad at my husband because they demanded he do something to save her. Blaming was always easier than facing the truth. The rude reality was there was nothing that could be done. They were not just losing a mother, he was losing a wife. It was an awful time in his family's life, and it was before my time with him, but I had to deal with some of the aftermath.

I began to dread when his son called because all they did was argue and it put my husband into what I referred to as "the blue funk." My husband went to bed for hours a day, sometimes several days in a row. He had promised their mother he would take care of the children. They weren't children anymore, they were adults. But his adult son took advantage of the promise and called up for handouts quite often.

I tried my best to explain that he was only enabling his son and his love and his money were two different things, support with love and respect, not with your money. His son would not get a regular job, and he drugged too much. You give me a drug addict, and I can give you an enabler. Whenever I tried to point this out, my husband snapped my head off, because he didn't want to believe his son was an addict. They blamed each other for their actions, and neither one was responsible for their own.

Communication and accountability were out the window when dealing with my husband's and his adult son's codependency. I felt like I was under attack with my husband's and his adult son's codependency. I had three choices fight, flight or freeze. I had already decided flight was not my choice. I was taught that fighting never solves anything, so freeze was the only choice left. Most of the time, I kept my mouth shut.

My husband cursed his adult son for being a musician. His son's talent was exceptional, but he rarely held a job because he was drug impaired. One day, trying to convince my husband to stop enabling, I said, "Sweetheart, it's not because he is a musician, if he were a plumber, he would still be unemployed. He has a drug problem." Telling someone something they don't want to hear causes some serious blowback. They both were in denial. I spent most of my time at the barn or in the bathtub.

Being a good mother under those circumstances was a challenge. I took my son to school every morning and picked him up every afternoon. I went on every school trip and chaperoned up until eighth or ninth grade when he felt grown up enough not to need his mom anymore. He asked me not to go. I respected his wishes. But many times, I could not keep our son from hearing the verbal abuse that went on in our household. I would call up a friend with children his age and work it out for us to go somewhere with them, so he and I could function in a healthy environment. I couldn't convince my husband not to yell with our son in the house.

I remember one time at the beach when our son was about ten and he and I were having a great time playing in the pool. There were couples around, and I have no idea what triggered this, but my husband demanded we get out of the pool and leave. Our son and I were having a boatload of fun. My husband exploded because we didn't move fast enough, and he began to create a scene. As quickly and quietly as possible, I swept my family out of the way, not to disturb everyone else enjoying their day. On that day, I couldn't have hated my husband more.

There was no greater backlash than when I tried to stop the purchase of a car for his drug-addicted son. My husband thought he was helping. Buying him a car as I saw it, allowed his son to spend his money on drugs. I gave in, supported my husband, and helped pick out a nice used car. His son quit a part-time deli job to get the car. He came home on the bus from Tennessee with his daughter, their clothes packed in a pillowcase. He left our house with a nice car, money to pay for taxes, licenses, and severance pay for having to quit his job to pick up his car. With that loot, he announced he deserved a vacation and was driving to Georgia to visit a friend. My husband and I were horrified. I looked at my husband.

"Stop this." I said.

"I can't do anything," he replied.

I thought, "Snatch the keys back!" His son went to Georgia, left his wallet, and had to drive many miles back. He arrived back in Tennessee and one day in his basement apartment for a drug related problem, his landlord evicted him and his daughter. They moved to a motel efficiency room that required pay per week. Soon, the thirty-day license expired and the money ran out. He traded down for a crummy car, so he could pay the fees. The whole episode was ludicrous, but this was the life of a drug addict.

In time, he and his daughter had nowhere to sleep but his car. He called home crying for help.

"Ok, you can come and live in the river cabin," his dad allowed. I thought this would be the turning point. We could put him in rehab, and we could provide stability for his daughter until he was drug free and ready to take over the responsibility. That was not what happened. For the next fifteen years, the chaos was the norm. I can't tell you how many ass chewings **I** got because **he** drugged, and **my husband** enabled.

When you are up to your eyeballs in sh**, sometimes, it is best to not to open your mouth. The dysfunction drugs and alcohol caused was almost overwhelming.

My horses and my girlfriends were my saving grace. I loved getting away to the horse shows for some much-needed fun. Under the load I was carrying, it was a miracle I got as far with my stallion as I did.

From the time my mom retired until she remarried at eighty, she was the most fun of all. Our antics were usually more fun than showing horses. No matter what we did, some mishap would occur, and we would laugh as we were the entertainment.

One horse show, I had two horses, one I rode and one she drove. I was braiding a ribbon in the horse's foretop while Mom held the ribbon. She always let it slide down, and I would have to do it over. I became aggravated when this happened.

"Hold this ribbon right here and no matter what, DON'T LET GO!" I snapped.

We started on this project, and the horse next door laid down and hit the stall. It startled the horse we were working on; the horse's head flew up and picked Mom up off the ground. She was holding on to the ribbon with all her might because I had just demanded she not let go. The horse slung her head sideways and flung Mom in the sawdust pile. In a few seconds, we were right back braiding the mane. In another moment...

"Ok, well, sometimes you can let go," I said. We burst out laughing. That was the birth of our version of Lucy and Ethel, two female comedians from the I Love Lucy TV show.

We were small women. When traveling, we strategically tried to keep ourselves safe. We stopped one night at a truck stop off the beaten path in pursuit of much-needed diesel. I pumped while Mom went in to pay. She didn't come out, and she didn't come out, and it was at night, what happened? I waited and waited and waited and finally got brave enough to investigate. I stepped in, and it was the land of giants! I am 5'4," and Mom is 5'1". The greasy spoon counter to my right had guys way over six feet tall and three hundred plus pounds. At the cash register was a giant too!

Where was Mom?! What have they done with her?! And what am I going to do about it?! I kept my head down and went to the restroom. No Mom! I came out, walked up and down the aisles and no Mom! I finally went back up to the register, and there was Mom. She had been there all the time, but the giant was obstructing my view. He was on the phone about a credit card, and she had been waiting all the time. What did we do? Got in the truck and laugh at the horror of a ridiculous, harmless situation. No matter what we did, it was funny, we laughed a lot, and we had fun. Our Lucy and Ethel antics were endless!

Now, years later, as I drove through Tennessee, where was this fun person, as opposed to the person who took the preacher's side, who committed me years ago and who recently tried to send me for anger management. WHO IS THIS PERSON? All I believed she was, was gone. Not only that, she forced me to take the action of kicking her out of my life. It honestly felt like she was dead. The Mom I thought I knew was gone. On top of the chaos with the church, I was grieving the loss of my mother. I needed to get away.

I rolled into my friend's farm. It had been more than twenty years since my last visit. At her request, I hopped in her SUV and she took me to see an addition to her farm where she had many broodmares and babies. She asked me if I was shopping for a horse.

"I couldn't care less about a horse, the reason I'm here is to see you," I replied.

I wanted to personally thank her for her support and encouragement she gave me with Mark whenever I asked. I gave her a heartfelt hug. She knew the big blow the loss of Mark was to me and I shared my losses were still piling up with the church and my mother. She listened and was supportive. She invited me to dinner, and we met a couple more horse friends. It was nice to talk horses over our meal and share a laugh. I left the next morning for Kentucky and planned to stop by again on my way home.

I didn't often travel through Tennessee to Kentucky, I usually went through West Virginia. The change of scenery was nice. I rolled into Lexington, and it felt like home. I knew the roads like the back of my hand. Why had I been away for so long? I drove deeper into Kentucky to spend a few days with another friend on his beautiful horse farm. I shared my heartbreaking story of losing my career horse. He told of his lost love, and together we found a little healing from sharing our grief. I was offered a job training on one of the most successful breeding operations in the business. The offer was another way I realized I had not lost all my success when I lost Mark. I started to realize people knew I had talent even though I thought my proof was gone. I was enjoying the visit.

I appreciated my friend's courteous manners, which I had never experienced in my marriage. I always liked watching my dad treat my mother with polite manners. My friend opened the car door for me, and he walked on the street side when we went down the street, and explained the custom started in the days of horse and buggy. If mud splashed, the gentleman would shield his lady from spoiling her dress. I smiled at the thought. As we walked out of the restaurant, I was in front, and proceeded to push the door open. "Whoa," he said, and I stopped in my tracks. Every horse person knew the term meant to stop. He stepped up and opened the door for me to go through. I chuckled and explained I knew polished manners, but I was not used to being treated that way. He opened the door and patiently waited while I got in the car. I thoroughly enjoyed the polite and respectful treatment.

The job offer came with housing, a nice salary, and commissions to boot. How inviting a geographical fix could be. I could walk away from all the chaos in my life and start over. What an offer to consider. My friend's recent courtship had failed because alcohol had taken its toll on their relationship. As a society, when will we ever learn?

I had a lot to think about on my trip back home by way of Tennessee. Should I take the job and leave my marriage and my son, who was about to turn fifteen. But what about **my** happiness? I had just drove away from peace and kindness and beautiful horses any horse trainer would dream of working. I thought about being stripped of the life I had made for myself many years ago. Do I want to go back home? For the second time in my life, I had lost everything I had worked for. Is the life I had built worth keeping?

I arrived at the motel in Tennessee and slept like a rock until eleven o'clock the next morning. All the miles thinking and running was totally exhausting. I stopped by to visit my friend and told her of the job offer. I was sick of being married and the only thing that wasn't worth leaving was my son. Maybe he would be fine without me.

I was tired of being a slave. I kept up the maintenance on the house and landscaping, my farm and horses, the river cabin, his retirement portfolio, and drove our son everywhere he needed to go. Juggling all my jobs plus watching the stock market every day, most all day, was enough to make anyone want to jump out the window. That chore was fit in between working horses. The *ss chewing for the stock market having a down day taught me to have nerves of steel. Why do I have to do it all?

I finally just sat and cried. My friend again listened and shared her wisdom that so many women had felt exactly the way I did. She shared her own story of grief. When she realized I couldn't see through my chaos, and I thought leaving my son was the answer, she gave me the dirtiest look I have ever seen and said, "GO HOME!"

I knew the answer anyway and headed home. But going home was harder than h*ll when I was emotionally beaten up and raw on the inside. I have never backed down from a challenge, but was this the time? A geographical fix would be easy. I was not the only woman who considered walking away from her marriage. Maybe I should have walked away years ago instead of trying to make it work. No one in my family had divorced, perhaps it was time I break the tradition. Maybe I didn't want to admit defeat, and I was unable to make my marriage work. I made a promise for sickness and in health until death do we part. Up until then, I had always kept my word.

Where do I go from here?

18

The Turn

Had it not been for my son, I don't think I would have looked back. I had stuck it out for this long, and I was not leaving until he graduated high school. The attraction to go to Kentucky was an incredible force to resist. Whenever I couldn't take the chaos anymore, I got in the car and drove to Kentucky, my land of escape. It was great to be able to get away from the monumental task of putting the pieces of my life back together.

One of the things I wanted to give our son was the knowledge of the courteous manners my Kentucky friend had showered on me. I wanted our son to be able to impress the girl of his choice with something as simple as manners do. They show respect. I suggested he learn more manners, and he took offense, like his father, when he misunderstood what I meant. Upset, he went outside with his dad following. I knew the conversation outside was not going the way I intended and went out to clarify. His dad stood between us, defending him as if I were a predator. My husband could take the littlest thing and turn it into a national disaster. I explained long enough to defuse the standoff, but the course in manners would have to be another day. If I left home, my son might go through an even bigger h*ll. I decided to stay and protect my son, but what was my course of action? For our son's last years at home, things needed to change.

If I was going to change things around in my son's life, I was going to have to turn things around in mine. If I had been able to complete the sale of my horse, I would have had a wad of money in my pocket to make the changes in my life. My business would have had capital, and I could have left the marriage if I had wanted and taken my son with me. I would have earned respect for the time I had dedicated to my horses, which was one of the things my husband badgered me about the most. I would no longer have to keep up the false front that our family life was peaceful and respectable. I was caught in the middle of codependent issues from drug and alcohol abuse to problems growing up suppressed. I didn't even begin to know the psychobabble used to describe it, nor did I care. All I wanted was peace and could someone please be kind to me. Was that so much to ask? What had I done to deserve people treating me this way?

Why not leave this mess and take my son with me? What was wrong with starting over? It wouldn't be the first time. Everything was set for me to step into a new, well paid job, complete with housing. I decided to pursue the opportunity a little further. My potential boss was so kind to me, I could had used the kindness. But suddenly, he shot himself in the foot when he politely insinuated I was to sleep with the boss as the job required. I was willing to let the relationship grow based on kindness, but a job requirement? I was not doing that. What a heartbreak. I had nowhere to go.

Please God, help me.

I had found God at the end of grieving for my horse, but since then, all I had done was to fight to keep my God. I realized I was put on this earth to use my God given talent for the good of creation and simply love one another. I just wanted to do God's will. The preacher wanted me to do his will, my mother wanted me to do her will, and my husband seemed to want to beat me down and a new boss dangled strings. You would think, after watching me suffer losing all that I had worked for, the people who supposedly loved me could do something besides just kick dirt in on me! What is it with all these ties? I don't think God put me on this earth for me to be a puppet or whipping boy! I HAVE HAD ENOUGH!

I put together the most professional sign proposal and mailed it to the church within the time allotted. I went to the session meeting and spoke my peace in the most professional way I could. It was the first time I had ever stood up to the establishment and politely told them they were wrong to run off a neighbor and my friend for a lighted sign. I walked out and didn't look back. I left with unbelievable hurt and at least one person on that governing session supported me during my presentation. She finally left too. Everyone else buried their head in the sand rather than face the fact the preacher was wrong. So what, he was only human.

Only God is perfect, the rest of us are far from it, that's why there is forgiveness. Are we called God's children because everyone is kicking, screaming and grabbing what we want? Are there any adults out there?

The farmhouse that initially went with my farm had been on the market for several months, and the lady who had lived there for many years invited me over to share her memories. When she showed me the bedroom where her beloved, deceased husband had spent his time during his illness, I knew the house needed to go with my farm. He positioned the bed to look out the window and watch the horses on my farm. I thought it would be a good investment. One, it would help the farm property value and two, I needed somewhere to go. My business finances were gone, but my husband could afford the investment. He gave me a check and agreed to put the house in my name. The farmhouse planted me in Virginia, so I wouldn't be tempted to run off to Kentucky, and I would continue to raise my son.

My Kentucky friend showed me enough kindness to know there was something out there better than how I had been living. I had found the passage in Proverbs: It is better to live in a rundown shack, than in a mansion with a petulant spouse. Maybe it was time for a change.

I was tired of fighting, I wanted peace, and this was it. The last straw came one day with my husband badgering me, and I stood up to him and felt forced to say, "I can't live like this anymore."

"Oh, YEAH? Do you want a DIVORCE? You'll take all my MONEY!" he said.

Money? Is that all he cares about? I wasn't going to strike a match to this unwanted fight. I wanted peace.

"I wouldn't dream of taking your money. It's so important to you. If you give me a little time, I will get on my feet," I said.

"Oh, YEAH? What are YOU gonna do?" he said.

I took one step back and thought, "This... is my partner?" I straighten my shoulders and leaned in.

"I, can train world-class horses, paint portraits or do photography. I'll THINK of something!" I said.

In all the years we had been married, I had never said I was leaving. My husband knew I wasn't kidding around. When I took the money off the table, he quickly realized it was me he was losing.

"Wh, wh, wh, whoa, whoa, wait a minute. Maybe we need a marriage counselor?!" he stuttered.

I leaned in again and squinted.

"YOU find one, and YOU go, and MAYBE I'll come," I said.

And he did it. He found one. After the first session, he came by the barn and asked me to lunch, which he rarely ever does. He informed me the counselor's specialty was in substance abuse. He realized he needed to solve his problem to keep his marriage. I wasn't sure I wanted the marriage, I just wanted to save myself and our son. In less than one year, I had lost my horse, my church, my mother, and maybe my husband. At least I found God.

The one person who supported me during my presentation to the Session appeared at just the perfect time, Laura. She was a Godsend. She invited me to her little upholstery shop in town, anytime I needed to talk. Funny how I found this place to light. I was so raw from being busted up, I needed to be recovered. We joked about her "therapy couch." She always had an antique couch she had refinished and was waiting to sell. I noticed a little frame on the table that said: "You need a good listening to." Best listener I had ever met. This time, I got lucky and fell into the right place for some healing support. Thank God, finally!

In the next two to three years, I kept myself busy, working. The physical work was not intellectually challenging, and I could examine the pieces. What can I build out of all this shattered debris of my life?

VI

Remounting
Life's Rough Ride

19

My Horses

I was ready to get back to work with my horses after I had returned from my trip out west. There were a lot of stages that I had gone through. I planned to start over. But the entire ordeal with the preacher and my mother blew me up so high, I refused to work a horse. I needed more time to get my anger and frustration under control.

One fellow horsewoman was a little frustrated with me because I spent so much time in the pool. Little did she know, I swam to keep in shape, so I could ride when I was ready.

"Are you back working yet?" another fellow horseman asked.

"Yes, I'm doing body work on my tractor," I replied. I knew what he was really asking, "Are you back working horses yet?"

"The problem with you is, you have too much talent," he said.

The real reason I dragged my feet so long in getting back to work was due to all the frustrations in my life, sometimes my pent-up anger got the best of me. I am ashamed to admit, on rare occasions, I took my frustrations out on my horses. In one sense, it was good I had an outlet because it kept me from taking it out on our son, as some parents do. The amount of work that goes with horses was good because, most often, I spent my energy working out my frustrations with things I accomplished. But on those rare occasions, I treated my horses precisely the same way some of the people around me treated me. If I couldn't get them to do what I wanted, in other words, control them, I used the whip harder than I should, or more lashes than ever should have been dished out. I tried to make them perfect. They sometimes broke into a sweat trying to survive being perfect as I thought they should. I know precisely how the horses felt. The people around me didn't physically whip me, but I did take my share of undeserved tongue lashings and unproductive criticism. And it seemed everyone had their way of wanting to control what I did. I was learning to set boundaries and everyone around me was learning what I meant when I said "No."

A better alternative in the past to whipping my horses was that I could cuss a blue streak. Tongue lash them, I did. I justified my cussing because it was at least better than a whip. But it did the same to horses as it did to children, induced more fear than ever belonged. Why was I taking my anger out on this horse when I was mad at my mother or furious with my husband? I refused to get back to work before I was sure I had my anger under control. It was three months after the breakthrough of the origin of my suppressed anger before I attempted to work the first horse. I spent days just rubbing on my horses and nothing else. I still wasn't sure if I wanted to continue in the business. I was angry with the horse business. Big business had stepped in and my fun had ended.

I had worked so hard and spent so much time learning and developing my farm property and breeding stock. Even if I wanted to quit, I had to get back to work to condition the horses to sell at a decent price. Getting back to work wasn't the question, it was when.

I did only what I liked, and if I didn't like it, I didn't do it. I couldn't stand dealing with a tail set. I went back to working My Lovely Lady, Amber for short. I showed her a few times with a natural tail, and the rulebook said: "set or unset tails." While showing on the clockwise way of the show ring, she flagged her tail on her own. At one show, she was mesmerizing, and everyone had their eyes on her! It added a new thrill to the ride, to sit in the middle of a show horse that was on the edge of exploding and the audience could see her excitement in more ways than one. We held together, and the ride was thrilling to take and to watch. I would like to say we won, but she had not yet settled to the excitement of the show ring under saddle, and we beat ourselves with a mistake on the last canter.

The next show, Amber had settled into the show ring excitement, and won with ease in an open class of twelve. I had her following in her father's footsteps. He had won in three divisions, and she had won two. I had caved into the pressure of setting and bracing her tail.

Something didn't feel right about bracing a tail. I felt as though I would rather quit showing than cut and brace another tail to show my horses. Why was that? I turned her out for both of us to have a break. She was so beautiful in my pasture; I decided for my enjoyment to raise a foal like her and her dad.

The wisdom the queen of the Saddlebreds came back again. "No one can ever take away what you know," she shared. I thought about what I had learned and acquired as a horsewoman. I didn't have a long list of world champions, only a few, or a who's who in a list of customers, like she did. But there was something to be said for working my horses and never having to answer to anyone else's deadline. They were ready when they were ready and so often, the slower I went, the faster I got there. I had the luxury of making my young horses into what they wanted to be.

Without the cash flow customers provided, I had learned to do a lot on my own. Farrier work was one of them. I had learned to make, punch, fit shoes and weld to put toe clips on the shoes I need. I had learned to balance a horse's foot, prevent unsoundness issues or correct them if they occur. I had learned all sorts of veterinary skills from caring for injuries, dispensing medications, orally, IM or IV, and even stitching up skin tears. I could palpate mares and breed by artificial insemination with fresh or frozen semen. I had collected semen, prepared it fresh and even frozen. I liked raising babies. Many legendary trainers had shared their training secrets.

I had learned to do a very fun thing and that was teach a horse to slow gait and rack. It was like teaching them to dance. First, I taught them to swing and then I taught them to step. One, two, three, four, one, two, three, four. When they really get good at it, the wind whipped past my ears. Whir Whir Whir Whir Whir Whir! It was so smooth, I rarely moved in the saddle. Then, my horse and I showed off what we knew and had fun.

Along the way, I adopted the Red Shirt Freshman, Fred, for short. He was a country pleasure horse that had won a Juvenile Reserve World Championship title and was about to be sold into harsh conditions. He had lived the life of a pampered show horse. I didn't think it was fair for a horse who had won such a high honor with a kid astride to go in that direction. He required no tailset, so I thought it was worth the try to turn around his issues and make a little money. Little did I know, he was going to assist in turning around mine.

I had been learning bits and pieces of dressage from a girlfriend who was an accomplished Grand Prix rider. Fred was angry, extremely nervous, and tense from years of mistreatment. My girlfriend and I decided he needed something entirely different. The sad thing about his treatment was, not that the people around him were evil or that Fred was either; his treatment amounted to about the same as happened to me. No one would listen, and everyone wanted to inflict their ways of control. Probably the best description was that he had PTSD, Post Traumatic Stress Disorder. I think it all started from an oddly shaped mouth in which no traditional bit fit correctly. I cut, welded and polished a custom-made bit to help solve his problem.

First, my close girlfriend and I worked together because she owed me for some hay work. After a few lessons, when payment was complete, my friend kept helping because she said she was doing it for Fred. A noble cause for a noble horse. She also knew Mark's loss had not only broken my heart, but also my bank account.

We used my girlfriend's way of training years before on another Saddlebred I had raised, so I had at least a clue of what she wanted. I felt as though what Fred and I were doing was ninety-five percent wrong and five percent right, due to all his issues. But a funny thing happened. She had criticized me over the years for my Saddlebred ways, but this time, things were different. She never said a word about what I was doing wrong, only what I was doing right. Sometimes she just stood and watched all the tension the horse displayed and my effort in dealing with him and would say, "I'm proud of you, I'm proud of you." It only made me want to try harder to get the result she wanted.

One day, my frustration escalated because of all of Fred's issues, and I was having a hard time trying to deliver the desired results. But this time I recognized when it got to a heated level. I stopped, dismounted my horse, handed the reins to my friend, and walked away. I was determined not to take my frustration out on the horse. I walked away to count to ten. At two, my frustration disappeared. My frustration was my frustration, no need to take it out on him. My girlfriend's tactic with the horse pointed out the same thing from a different view. "That's his stuff, stay out of it." I was responsible for my actions, and he was responsible for his. I stopped walking away, turned around, and mounted my horse.

I think what sounded so great about "I'm proud of you," was that finally, someone in this world was proud of me for what I WANTED TO DO and not what someone else wanted me to do. Our work was just strictly for the common goal of rehabilitating Fred, with no negative energy. To hear encouraging words was music to my ears.

On my own, I practiced long and hard between lessons to again achieve her praise. A couple of days later, I woke up with such pain in my back; I could barely get out of bed. I was sure I had ruined my riding career. Eleven years earlier, I had herniated a disc while working with a difficult horse and had a lumbar laminectomy, but this was different. After a visit to the radiologist for an x-ray, and a solid week of Ibuprofen day and night, I was back in the saddle again. My heart and determination were getting stronger.

The most significant change in what my girlfriend was trying to teach me and what I had learned before was not to force a horse into a frame but to teach him to hold his frame. I looked at it as the same as teaching children. You don't control them; you show them how to control themselves. I was learning a new technique of communicating with a horse instead of controlling them. It was a lesson for me in the personal growth of giving up control to gain control.

Winter was about to roll around and my girlfriend went back to Florida as always. I started to experiment with my own technique. I wanted to see if I could get my horses to work for me the same as I wanted to work for her. Since it was the end of show season, I decided to start over. Could I put the power of kindness to work?

How easily communicating with a horse came to me because my anger was no longer boiling just below the surface. I whispered colts to ride and drive in no time. Since I didn't like dealing with tail sets, I sold all my young stock that would soon require wearing one.

It was remarkable what I could get a horse to do, yet with no physical connection to him, no bridle, no saddle, no lines, just me and the horse. I asked them to walk, trot, canter, stop, turn around and come to me. My theory worked like a top. I was practicing giving up control to gain control. I set boundaries and built a relationship with each one. Each horse looked forward to his daily workout. It was precisely the same as dealing with them as my instructor had dealt with me.

I rehabilitated Fred while he rehabilitated me. I took him back to the show ring, and he showed me how much he fought his ghosts. I could relate. I see how people have such a bad experience at something they have trained for, that they never want to do it again. Fred seemed to feel the same way about the clockwise direction of the ring; he tried to come unglued and almost did. Even though I had been out showing the year before with Mark's daughter, Fred was the exact color as Mark, and it brought out my lingering feelings of grief. At the showgrounds where I had not shown Mark, I was fine. But the show rings where I had such fun with Mark, gave me that shell-shocked feeling all over again. I guess the horse and I both had emotional trauma. Remnants of a broken heart would be a better description for me.

At one showground very familiar to Mark and me, right before I mounted to show, I sat and shed tears to rid myself of that awful shell-shocked feeling. I had never been one to shed tears, but I sometimes discovered tears were an excellent way to cleanse the soul. I stepped in the stirrup, mounted my horse and went on to win the class. And thank God for Beverly, one of my dearest girlfriends, who helped and supported like she always did.

Since it was easier for me to go somewhere different, I decided it might be easier to get Fred in the show ring by doing something different. I taught him to carry the American flag which gave him something else to think about doing. We went his stressed-out direction in the ring but did something different. I called on my friend, Peyton, the show manger, to let me carry the flag during the National Anthem, and he agreed if I would show him at practice that Fred could do it. So, with music and all, we showed him what we could do. Peyton agreed. Fred and I carried the flag at the beginning of two nightly sessions, and I showed him in a regular class the last night. Each time I rode him in the ring doing something different, the more relaxed he became. The idea worked.

All horses are trainable, and all people are redeemable. We were working hard.

My flag ride with Fred was videoed and, since he suffered from PTSD like some US soldiers, I turned the video to honor service men with A Memorial Day Salute on the Mark of Design LLC channel on YouTube. Was this my last time in the showring?

I finally realized what didn't feel right about setting and bracing a horse's tail. I knew exactly what it was like to be running free, caught, held against my wishes, and forced to receive whatever treatment the people responsible for my care thought well to administer. I cannot do the same to a lovely horse. I would not set and brace a horse's tail again. I wouldn't want my tail cut. Even if the surgery is skipped, I cannot stretch the tail muscles with a tailset and force them to sleep in leather straps all their show careers. If I decide to show my horse under the rules of a set or unset tail, will my horse be judged fairly?

Was it time I move on to something else?

20

My Fifth Broken Heart

My girlfriend was very dear to me to step in and help me with a new way of working Fred. Our friendship spanned more than a decade. It started when she bought a Saddlebred from me years ago. We shopped, we rode horses, we traveled, we decorated, we made grape jelly, we laughed and laughed a lot. She participated in our annual family reunion for so many years during the Hillsville Flea Market and she had become one of the family. She was more than a close girlfriend: she was like my big sister. For a time, we were inseparable, everyone was used to seeing us together. When the rest of my world was falling apart, she helped in calming my storm.

When I lost my horse, my girlfriend had lost her mother and husband. She knew my horse and accomplishments and I knew her mother and husband. We shared our grief. She was there when the church and my mother turned on me. It was in her kitchen that my explosion occurred. She saw the relationship with my husband and commented on how kind I could be when he could be such an ass. She shared her own horror story that a divorce could be awful. We grew up in different circumstances, yet we were so much alike and, in some ways, entirely different. While her husband was still living, I watched her sometimes roar at him like a lion. It wasn't exactly the way I was taught to handle the situation, but my quiet approach wasn't working either. Neither of our husbands understood what "no" meant.

All the things I had been leaning on were gone except my close girlfriend. I was working hard at finding my footing, but I depended on her more than I realized. Her life wasn't perfect either and she started to snap at me for things in the past of which I had no control.

I tried to help in her problem, only to create a problem between us that didn't exist before. It was the same thing my mother had done to me. The fear of losing someone so loved came out as desire for control.

The spark that ignited the friendship blowup came when she said, "Why would I want to hear..." What I heard was, "I'm not going to hear you..." That misunderstood comment, unknowingly to both of us at the time, stuck a red-hot poker in the reopened wound caused twenty-five years earlier. At that time, my life took a fateful turn when my mother refused to hear a word I said and took control of my life. It was a deep wound and a buried issue that had only surfaced a few months before. It was hard for me to interpret and take control of my intense, raw emotions. Defending myself created words that cut at my friend. My poor choice of words, in addition to her anger, blew us up so high, my big sister wouldn't talk to me for months. So high, our cat fight caused my adopted big sister to skip the summer coming to Virginia. At least, it was a civilized cat fight because we didn't need teeth or claws to kill. Words were enough.

When Mom asked me where was my friend that summer, I had to tell her we had a sisters' spat. My mom wasn't happy with me because I broke the big family rule of no fighting. No matter where I went, I was in trouble. The furnace of affliction was setting my *ss on fire in Virginia while Sissie spent the summer burning in h*ll in Florida!

I couldn't paint a better illustration that no matter where we ran, we couldn't get away from ourselves.

"I'm never spending another summer in Florida!" she announced first step in the door at the family reunion.

Mom held **me** completely accountable for our spat, while it wasn't entirely my fault. I had to work hard to patch things up by flea market time, so the 'good sister' didn't miss the annual family reunion. We were way too much like sisters, because this was the same as getting in trouble with my brother! I was always the scapegoat!

FIFTY YEARS of fighting with my brother couldn't hold a candle to one knockdown, drag out battle with a sister! How did I get here? If this was the dark side of sisterly love, I needed a flashlight! This was definitely the wrong path!

Please God, deliver me from this Worrell family!

What was different with this relationship than the others were that we had a bond, not a tie. We had bonded like sisters, yet, we were only very close girlfriends. She had the choice of never coming back. I never suffered denial from Mark's death. I knew from the moment he died, he was never coming back. The church didn't explode, it was still standing and technically I was still a member. Once a mother, always a mother, we would always have a tie. Unless divorce was the option, my husband and I had legally tied a knot. The loss of my girlfriend was the even harder than losing Mark because she was still on this earth. Would she ever come back? The **not knowing** was the heaviest load I had to bear. Coming on top of all my other losses, this was my fifth broken heart in less than a year. Would I even survive? Did I even want to? Was there nothing left?

My entire life blew up starting with the death of one horse. How could this happen? Was he only just a horse? God, help me!

"When I get through all these broken hearts---bullets will bounce off my chest," I said to another friend on the phone one day. Is it true what doesn't kill you will make you grow stronger?

I learned many things from this mistake. I could have helped my sister/girlfriend in a stressful time if I had just listened and given my two cents when she asked like I have done so many times before. There was a difference in providing support as opposed to controlling someone else's life.

An adopted "sister". One that is let "in" so close, tells the truth whether it's wanted to be heard or not. Truthfully, maybe one should be called an "Insister."

But isn't that the way the world seems to work? Everybody is talking, and nobody is listening. Why is everyone trying to solve someone else's problem? Can I just save myself?

When my girlfriend wouldn't talk to me anymore, I had nowhere to dump the garbage from my marriage. I ended up dumping my husband problem where it belonged which was back on my husband. He needed to deal with his issues. I realized I was dumping on my girlfriend instead of solving my problem. It was my problem and it was up to me to solve it. I had tried everything I knew to get through to my husband, and finally I tried what worked for her and that was to roar like a lion. It wasn't fun for my husband or me, yet it did stop his hurtful words.

Roaring was a woman's right and, as a woman, I had a license to be bipolar. Quietness didn't work, so I tried anger. The chaos in my household had reached an unacceptable level for years. I think at one time or another most women come home to chaos, march in, and loudly announce, "I HAVE HAD ENOUGH!" And if not, maybe they should. I guess I was a slow starter. But anyway, my girlfriend taught me a new tactic. I was desperate for peace.

I had no idea how buried issues were a hidden monster which reared its ugly head and struck at people or opportunities most important in my life. No wonder no one wanted to look within and open a festering wound. It was painful. But to really heal, there was no way around it. I was very willing to open and let out hurt, so I could have closure and peace.

Almost two years passed before the friendship truly began to recover from the rocky road of my journey. I have never worked so hard at repairing a friendship/sisterhood in my life. In the future, I plan on never blowing one up again.

How could I have been so stupid as to blow us up? The same way my mom could be so insensitive as to commit me for a broken heart. We both thought taking control was the answer. I was desperate for my girlfriend/sister to forgive me the same as my mom was desperate for me to forgive. How could I not forgive my mother for something I had just done myself?

Why do we not realize how precious people are until after they are gone?

I thought about the kindness my girlfriend/big sister had shown while working with me and my horse. It brought me back to what Granddaddy wanted to tell me of the French girl he had met during the wars. Now I understood what he was trying to tell me: When you have marched through a living hell and there was a woman on the other side who was kind to you, there were no words to express the gratitude. There was no power in the world as great as the power of kindness, especially when I needed it most. No wonder Granddaddy went all the way from England to France to see his kind French girl again. Was this how God intended sisterly love to be?

My 'kind' sister pointed out I was getting older and if I wanted freedom and power, I had better get started. She was right. I had a long road ahead.

VII

Standing Up,
Shaking Off the Dust,
and Rebuilding

21

My Farmhouse Retreat

I wish I could say the marriage counselor was the solution to our problem, but it wasn't that easy. I sat in **my** house, which was in **my** name to decide how I wanted to proceed with **my** life. I didn't know if things would change with my husband. Our problems had existed for years.

Did I want to stay married? What did I want to do with this house? Did I want my mother back in my life? Did I want to go back into the horse business? Why did the people of my granddaddy's church team up against me? Will my friend ever come back? I can hear so many questions in the quiet of my retreat. The silence was deafening.

I looked around at the inside of this house. It needed work. It would give me something to do, while I thought about what direction to take my life. I realized if the answer to everything was to walk away, at some point, there was nothing left. I decided to take a stand for what I wanted. The one thing I was unwilling to give up was my son.

For right now, I was not moving in this house. The highlight of my day was driving my son to school and spending those few minutes alone, just he and I. In another year he would be driving, and I was not missing out on our private time together. Ever since he came into this world, I rarely had private time at home with him because my husband was standing over us. I had to take him away from home for mom and son fun time together. His dad's dysfunction could ruin fun almost every time. I worried if I left, things would be harder for my son.

Every morning, I took my son to school, went to the barn to work my horses, and worked on my farmhouse. When I came home, supper was ready. We quietly ate together. I tried to make it where there wasn't any time for an argument. I used the solace of the bathtub and went to bed. My husband was working with the marriage counselor, and things seemed to be quiet. Not entirely peaceful, but better.

While I worked on my house, I had plenty of time to think about all the things that went wrong. Many problems could have been solved so simply with good communication and accountability. What if the preacher, when I asked him why he didn't do his job of supplying the copy, had said, "You know you are right, let's get on it." It would have saved a mountain of grief and hurt. What if I didn't snap back with the comment, "I had to dig deeper into my pocket to pay his salary?" I would not have ignited his anger. What if many years ago, when I went for a walk and came home, my mom had said, "Sweetheart, this is so unlike you. What's wrong?" My heartbreak would have come out and a mother's hug would have healed what ailed me. I would have gone right back to Kentucky and continued my life I had made for myself. But if I had, I wouldn't have had my son.

The most significant realization with my marriage was the problem was half my fault. I had been trying to solve my husband's issues the same as my mother tried to solve my problem. I was part of the problem. I thought our marriage problems were his fault and he thought they were mine. In retrospect, we were both were right. It was my fault I let his prior family's dysfunction come into my marriage, so I quit trying to solve his problems, and solve my own. It was his fault to bring his prior family problems and his issues into his new family.

Nothing had made me madder than to be held responsible for things over which I had no control. I had this realization years earlier, but nothing I said seemed to make my husband understand. I came up with these statements, and they worked somewhat. Whenever he would dump his problems on me, I would say something like this, "Well you know I control the weather, I don't know how I let that slip by me." Or sometimes I would say, "I don't control the world, and I don't control that either." I refused to take on his problem. I did try my best to get him to quit enabling his adult son and support him with his love and encouragement. Most times they argued, I ended up the whipping boy.

Every day I spent hours and hours refurbishing my ninety-seven-year-old farmhouse, plastering the seams of the wallpaper and sanding the edges smooth so they wouldn't show through the paint. It helped me in so many ways. Having something to do was therapeutic along with hours of silence. I gained more understanding of myself and my life.

I was trying to get past the enormous anger I had for my husband. Ten years earlier, I told him that "I was not living like this anymore." He asked if I wanted a divorce. "I didn't say anything about a divorce. I said I'm not living the next ten years like the last ten years." The dysfunctional codependent relationship with his adult son and his granddaughter wreaked havoc on our lives.

My husband quoted from AA numerous times, "The definition of insanity is doing the same thing over and over and expecting a different result." I wanted to break the chaos. Let's try something different.

The topic of this story with his adult son and granddaughter could fill another book. We tried different things, and each gained a little ground, but it didn't end the enabling like it needed to. I finally used the same method that my stepson and step-granddaughter used to keep getting handouts. I called it the wear down tactic. They went on and on and on until he gave in. My husband and I had made many deals with each other, that his most recent enabling effort would be the last, and my husband always broke his word.

About five years ago, we made the last deal with my husband to cut the apron strings with his adult son and I meant it. Of course, my husband went back on his word, and I set the wear down tactic in motion. I harped on him every day the enabling was to stop. Living with the "wearer downer" was more than he could take. I finally won out. He did it. The strings were cut.

Ever since then, his son has been supporting himself with his musical talent, and his granddaughter is in nursing school. I am quite proud of them both. They are standing on their own two feet and learning to take care of themselves.

Now, I had my own house. The place we lived in was my husband's house before I came into the picture. Our plans going into our marriage were to buy some land and build a house and barn on the same piece of property. After we married and were shopping for land, he changed his mind and didn't want to move. I felt he broke his promise. I made the best out of what was available. He financed the barn I built on my mother's property. I drove thirty minutes to the barn and thirty minutes back every day and sometimes two or three times a day for years. Then he complained that I spent too much time away from home. If he had done as he promised, I would have been close all the time.

Early in our marriage, he begged me to give up taking in customer horses. Their horses would demand a lot of my time training and taking them to horse shows. I thought long and hard about what he was asking. I would have to work ten times harder for a fraction of the money he was making at the time. My husband's deal sounded like a good idea for quality of life. I chose to put family first.

"Ok, I'll make a deal with you. If you buy me three broodmares and pay breeding fees, I'll give up taking in customer horses," I said. "I can raise and train my own stock."

"Ok." He agreed.

Mark and others were the product of my breeding program. It took a few years to find the right crosses. Our accountant liked the write off on the years I was in the red. The only way I could make money was to sell my homebred horses. I had sales, but nothing like the deal I had pending with Mark. I was about to take off with the sale of Mark sometime after my husband's retirement. He pressured me about when the transaction with Mark would be complete. I was worried about the well-being of my horse, and he was harping about the money. I reminded him of the deal we made not to have customer horses, or there would have been cash flow. Why was everything all about money? Why was I responsible for everything when WE made a deal? Couldn't he take some responsibility?

At the beginning of owning this farmhouse, he marched in and told me that we would need to enlarge the kitchen and add on to the bedroom. I liked the charm of the house as it was, and I didn't think it was gonna be WE, I think it was gonna be ME. I didn't say a word. In time, I asked him one day, "How many houses have you owned?" He rattled off several towns and such, and the total came to seven.

"Well, this is the very first house of my own, and I would like to do it as I please," I said.

I reminded him that the farmhouse was in my name. I think he realized "our" house was in both our names. I don't think he wanted to pick that fight, and neither did I. I never wanted to fight. This farmhouse was my haven, and I intended to keep it that way.

His marriage counselor helped him understand my point of view. I finally agreed to go see her. I spent much of my time filling out her paperwork and she wanted to be paid in cash. It cost me over one hundred dollars for her time to listen to me. I explained I wanted to give some background before I got to my husband. As I spoke she interrupted.

"Wait, I haven't got to my point yet," I said.

She interrupted, and she interrupted, and she interrupted. When I finally got to where I wanted to be, her comment was that she and my husband thought that I should do such and such. What kind of therapy session was that? I felt like exploding, she made me so angry. I told her to tear up all that paperwork, and I was never stepping foot in her office again. Truthfully, she was lucky I wasn't a violent person. I gave her an "F" in bedside manner.

I thought long and hard on the way home to figure out why I got so mad. I realized she did exactly what the hospital psychiatrist had done to me twenty-five years ago: interrupted and decided my life for me. No wonder I got so mad. But take away the anger, if I didn't like a service I was paying for, I didn't have to go back. No anger needed. Problem solved.

My power is growing.

Christmas was upon us, and my husband and I decided the only thing we were going to do was buy our son a quality guitar. I wanted peace, and my husband had everything he wanted, so we didn't plan on exchanging gifts. Our son was playing in the youth praise band, and my friend, the director, said it was time he stepped up to a better-quality instrument. She informed me where to shop out of town, who to talk to before I went shopping and spend at least five hundred dollars for the quality of the instrument. I spoke to the people and found the right stores. My family made a plan for our Christmas to go to at least three different music shops, narrow the choice to three guitars and pick one. Going for the outings and eating out together was our Christmas celebration.

I was working late one day on my farmhouse and, while sanding plaster, my husband called. He announced he had taken my son to the guitar shop in town, found a guitar, and bought it. I couldn't believe what I had heard. He knew I was going to be mad and tried to justify his decision that it had only cost three hundred and fifty dollars. That only added fuel to the fire.

I decided right then I had had enough. This was the day I was going to stand up to him for always breaking his word. I was about to unloaded countless years of anger for never wanting to fight within earshot of our son. This time it didn't matter because I was taking up for our son. I had a thirty-minute trip to cool off and the drive time had no cooling effect on my anger. I was finally going to direct my anger at the very person who deserved it.

When I walked in the door, he took one look at me and knew he was in deep sh**. He started to defend himself.

"Now, now, now, you always get mad when I make a decision without you..." He stuttered.

"SO, WHY, DO YOU DO IT!" I blasted! He started to stutter his reply and I never gave him the chance.

"IF IT ONLY COST $350, IT IS NOT QUALITY ENOUGH! WE HAVE BOUGHT COUNTLESS CHEAP INSTRUMENTS TO FIND THE ONE HE TAKES TO, AND THIS IS IT! FURTHERMORE, THIS PROCESS OF BUYING THIS GUITAR WAS OUR ENTIRE CHRISTMAS CELEBRATION, AND YOU THREW IT AWAY WITH YOUR IMMEDIATE GRATIFICATION! THAT'S ALL YOU TAUGHT YOUR OTHER SON WAS IMMEDIATE GRATIFICATION! I WANTED **MY SON** TO KNOW SOMETHING A LITTLE DIFFERENT!" I roared!

Thank God my husband had enough sense to know not to tangle with a roaring lion! He said the owner would gladly take the guitar back.

"THAT'S GOOD BECAUSE THAT IS WHERE IT'S GOING!" For the first time, **I am woman hear me roar** and this lion was protecting her cub! Before, I must have whispered or whimpered because it seemed I was never heard. I think he knew better than to mess with a roaring lion and for **once**, he shut up.

This incident gives me a new perspective on the well-known Bible story of Daniel in the lion's den. Daniel had enough sense to keep quiet and pray. Does it always take threatening men within an inch of their lives for them to figure out to leave sleeping lions in peace?

I went in to tell my son about the change in the guitar. I sat down beside him, knowing he had heard the whole thing. Before I said a word, he looked over at me with the biggest ear to ear grin I have ever seen. I knew what that meant. So many times, when I was growing up, I thought, "Why does my mom put up with my dad's crap?" Now, I can say my dad's crap was unsolved anger issues.

My son had heard the verbal abuse going on for years. And this was a lot worse than my dad ever gave. I guess when you grow up with verbal abuse, you learn to tolerate it and that was the problem. We were taught never to tolerate physical abuse, not to mention sexual abuse. I never did. I wish I had learned not to endure verbal abuse. I had heard enough!

I explained to my son we were prepared to spend between five hundred and a thousand dollars for his electric guitar and how proud I was that he had developed his talent to earn one. His smile didn't go away, and it was the brightest light I have ever seen. He got up from his computer chair, said "Thanks Mom" and topped it off with the biggest of hugs! I wondered if putting his dad in his place ranked over the guitar, but both were a grand day for him. And me too.

I went into the bathroom to clean up from my day of roaring and farmhouse work. I looked in the mirror and, to my horror, my hair was white on top and gray all around! I wasn't gray this morning! I looked like a ninety-year-old hag. I had no idea what I looked like when I was shouting at my husband. He must have thought, "Where did this witch come from?" I thought, "Oh my! This is making me age way before my time." The next glance in the mirror and I couldn't help but chuckle. My instant aging was the result of plaster dust from sanding the walls in my house. I couldn't get in the shower fast enough to wash it all away. I laughed. I won!

For the first time in many years, the verbal abuse had stopped. We had fun shopping for the guitar, and we all agreed on a beautiful used Gibson. The face was a metallic blue, swirled with silver. It looked like water. The salesman explained the Gibson factory had flooded some years ago and was shut down for six months. This color combination commemorated the reopening.

Our son was excited to take it to his youth band practice and I watched as he unveiled his treasure to his friends. They were terrific in sharing his excitement. I wouldn't trade that moment for the world!

I worked and worked on my farmhouse retreat. I hired the most talented carpenter, whom I had met in choir. He brought his friend as his assistant, and the three of us got along perfectly. Funny how whatever I needed showed up in perfect time. I was lucky to catch him in between jobs. We met in the mornings to discuss the job, and I went on to building a fence on the farm. At times, I came in at lunch, and whenever I wanted to talk, he patiently sat and listened and shared some wise advice. Finding God was a journey and how one wise person can guide another was something special to experience.

If I could envision it, they could build it. They stated working for me was easy because I knew what I wanted. It was nice working with men so easy to get along with because I found it almost impossible to do anything easy with my husband. He was quick to get defensive no matter how anything was said. But my husband did point out the improvements were a good investment and he willingly helped financially. Thank God, occasionally we could constructively get along.

I enjoyed finding treasures to decorate in the farmhouse flavor. My close girlfriend and I often went on treasure hunts and found gems in the most fun and unexpected places. I lucked into several treasures next door at The Barn Shop. The owner sometimes called when she found a unique treasure she thought I would like.

I had everything decorated, but the last room, I dreaded. I had planned a trophy room for Mark. I gathered and piled his things on a table centered in the front room. When I started putting his pictures in the frames, shoes, and halter in the shadow box and trophies on the wall, I was surprised that the exercise was therapeutic. Upon completion, I invited friends to admire it. It was interesting how solemn they were, and sometimes they couldn't help but wipe away a tear. I appreciated that they shared my grief. In no time, I found myself happy to share my fun with Mark instead of my loss. What I once dreaded, helped me work toward closure. The front room ended up as a tribute to the horse who changed my life; "The Mark Room."

My farmhouse became the cornerstone in my rehab along with building fences. I worked hours upon hours putting the vision of my farm and farmhouse together.

During all this physical labor, I searched within myself and sometimes all the way back to my childhood to find a piece to my inner puzzle.

I was determined to sort through the pieces of my broken life and build something better.

22

My Parenting Skills

On the top of my list was our son. I realized many times; I was busy trying to tell him what to do, instead of listening to what he had to say, and what he needed. After the rude awakening from what happened to me, my parenting skills took a major turnaround. Anywhere I tried to control what he did, I quickly quit that tactic. I kept on with giving him consequences for his actions but controlling him died a quick death. My communication skills became much kinder and I made sure I heard everything he had to say.

One day, I heard him say, loud and clear, "Mom, you already told me that!" It made me think back to when I heard from my parents the same thing over and over again. "Do they think I'm stupid or something!" I thought back then. I knew my son wasn't stupid, so I started telling him what I wanted him to know as clearly as I could, and I only said it once. Whenever a teachable moment came up, I would start by saying, "The lesson for today is..." He quickly learned I was only going to say it once, and he would stop what he was doing and gave me his undivided attention. How many people could say their teenager was a captive audience? My parenting skills were growing and getting easier.

Changing the relationship with him was easy because I was in the power position. The more I lessened my authority and got on his same level, the better communication and the better the result. I quit treating him as if I had power over him, treated him more as an equal, and honestly heard what he had to say.

The object of the parenting game is to raise children into adults, so they are responsible for their actions and can take care of themselves.

I have a little more than two years before he legally becomes an adult. There is so much I want him to know, but I realize, as a parent, I cannot teach him a lifetime of experience in just eighteen years. I concentrate on what I think is most important and take advantage of any teachable moment that presents itself. I phrase it that he is becoming a great man and I am going to give him tools for his man bag. Respect, integrity, kindness, trustworthiness, accountability and the much-needed skill, the ability to communicate.

I realized he was doing the same thing I had done all my life when tensions got tight. Freeze. As I was growing up, we were taught backtalk to our parents was disrespectful. In stressful times, I learned to keep my mouth shut. I didn't want my son to grow up with the same fate. I wanted him to talk back to me. I wanted him to learn better communication skills.

This was today's lesson...."I know you're frustrated, and not talking is not an option. Tell me that you are frustrated and tell me what you are frustrated about, " I said. First, his words came out a little heated and the longer he talked, and I listened, the calmer he got. There's not been a problem in communication since.

He had failed his written driver's test twice. He couldn't get through identifying ten signs. One, he didn't study enough and two, the time he spent traveling in the car, while growing up, was spent watching a video or playing an electronic game. Those devices won over looking out the window and observing road signs.

When summer was upon us, I asked him to work at the barn to help with his future car insurance. I took him to the driving range at the high school and taught him to drive my manual car. He had his learner's permit, and he drove to and from the barn to work with me. He cleaned stalls, groomed horses and learned to ride his horse, Jack. I quizzed him on the signs everywhere we went. By the end of the summer, he passed his driver's test and got his permanent license. He was pleased.

"This was the best summer ever," he said. I was delighted with both of us.

When I quit trying to control what he did, parenting was more relaxed, and we started having more fun. While working upstairs in the farmhouse one day, I asked him if he would help me paint a bedroom.

I couldn't make up my mind between tan or yellow as he walked in the room.

"Yellow. All the downstairs is tan," he said.

So yellow it was. I had a drop cloth all over the carpet, and I had been rolling paint on with a roller that stores paint on the handle. I could refill the roller without stopping. He had used it before, and I handed it over to him and went downstairs to do other work. After a while, I came up to see how he was doing.

"I'm finished! How does it look?" he said.

I surveyed all around. He had paint on his face, in his hair, on his arms and he had stripped down to his skivvies not to get it on his favorite shirt and pants, but his skivvies did pay the price. The paint was all over the drop cloth. The actual paint job on the walls looked great.

"You did a great job!" I said, with the greatest grin. I'm so sorry I didn't get a picture of him.

"Thanks, Mom! I'm going to wash my hands and go home," he said, with a big smile.

I knew if I had scolded him for the mess, he would end up frustrated at working and he wouldn't want to help me again. Most importantly, he had done a **good job**. I loved his stick-to-it-ness! There was just a little more cleanup than usual.

Every horseman or woman knows that if you fall off a horse, you get right back on. With my skill of training horses and instructing, my son has never hit the ground.

I had taught him to waterski, and while out with some friends, he took a tough fall. Tough love set in on that day.

"I know that hurt, but I'm not letting you back in this boat until you get back on those skis. You can ask Mom. She wrecked her bicycle, skinned her knees and didn't get back on. She has regretted it ever since. If you quit now, the fall is all you will remember. You get back up on those skis and, in time, you will hardly remember the fall." I coached.

Upset I wasn't very sympathetic, he gritted his teeth and skied like a man on a mission. He still loves to ski. The lesson paid off, he learned perseverance.

He got accepted to Governor's School and often, at the dinner table, he liked to impress us with what he had learned.

"Do you know that fifteen percent of snails that are eaten by birds survive?" he asked.

"No, I didn't," I said.

"So, is that how those snails get planted?" his dad added.

Our son and I looked at each other with a grin but puzzled.

"Planted? What do you think grows if a snail gets planted? I asked.

"Two snails?" his dad replied.

My son and I looked at each other and burst out laughing.

"Don't you wonder how you made it into Governor's School?" I asked.

We broke into laughter. Our home life was happier and turning around for his remaining time with us before college.

I laughed at his mistakes instead of browbeating him for doing something wrong. He learned to laugh at himself. I wanted him to be able to tell me anything because things in life don't always go right and friends his age don't always give the best advice. He once told me, on the way home from my mom's house, how he and his cousins were in the basement trying peach brandy that one cousin had supplied. I laughed at what they were up to and it set up the perfect teachable moment about drinking and peer pressure. He heard every word.

I pointed out a story on the evening news about fraternities with hazing and drinking deaths. He said that was why he wasn't interested in joining. That was one solution. If that was what he chose for himself, that was the one I would respect.

I am quite proud of the young man he has become. I hope and pray he stays safe. Ever since he has had his own car, his safety is out of my control. He did have one traffic incident. It was a significant teachable moment. He had gotten an internship at his college of choice. He asked me one morning if he could travel on the interstate instead of the less traveled two-lane road.

"I don't know about that. Ask your dad," as I deferred.

He left and made the executive decision to do it anyway. A policeman pulled him over for going eighty-two MPH in a sixty-five MPH zone. He thought the exit was shortly ahead and he slowed down but continued to the exit. He miscalculated, and the ramp was three miles ahead. When he finally pulled over, the policeman was angry and jerked his arm while he was trying to get his wallet out. That scared him to death. The policeman gave him speeding, reckless driving for fifteen MPH over the limit and failure to yield. He called home to tell us, and he was so upset that he asked his dad if he could come home. His dad asked my opinion.

"Tell him to go on to his internship. He was in such a hurry to get there anyway. We'll deal with it when he gets home," I said. He went on to his course.

My son was scared to face me. I was so glad his first incident didn't result in his car crashing into a tree.

"Well, you pay the consequences. You're going to have to pay for fees, a lawyer, and do whatever the court says," I told him.

"I'm ok with that," he agreed quickly.

He put in early to get a job at the city pool and got it. He paid the lawyer, fees, court costs, and had to do fifty-five hours of community service. It worked out very well because, sometimes, he did drive too fast. This ticket solved the speeding problem, and the consequence was that his earned money went somewhere besides his pocket. Nobody likes that.

He learned he was not above the law and his parents were not going to pay to get him out of trouble. Since then, he has no problem sticking to the speed limit. What the real-world hands over is consequences for his actions, just like his parents.

On the way home from the barn one day, he was chattering and chattering, and we stopped for a cone of frozen yogurt. He sat across the booth from me telling about the rudeness of this friend to her parents and the parents' treatment of another friend. His chatter abruptly stopped.

"Thank you for being such a cool parent. I'm glad I'm not like that," he said.

Knock me over with a feather! As a parent, that was a **slam dunk!**

I started thinking about the influence of my own parents.

VIII

Culling and Taking Stock
of My Past Life

23

My Mother and Father

My mom and I had lots of fun together. We enjoyed riding horses and going to horse shows together. We shopped, laughed and shared funny stories. Dealing with what my mother had done to me twenty-five years ago and the reality that she was ready to do it again was the hardest thing I have ever had to face in my life.

When I lost Mark, he was gone from this earth and never coming back. But the mother who I had known was gone, yet the person I thought I knew so well and trusted wholeheartedly remained on this earth. Who was this person who had been everything to me and my best friend for decades? What was she thinking?

I have never been able to understand how people fall out with their mothers and never want to see them again. They don't talk to their mothers anymore, don't allow them in their lives, or argue all the time with them. I never fought with my mother.

Now I understand how those other people feel. Never in a million years did I think that I would be one of them.

I finally decided I would go to a therapist since my mother was adamant that I needed a grief counselor or a doctor. But before the appointment rolled around, I thought, "That's no reason to go...because my mother wanted it." I started to cancel the office visit, but then I decided I would go for myself. I told the therapist what had happened with all my losses and being committed by my mother. She asked me a few questions, and, at the end of the hour, she said, "You don't have any issues, but there is something wrong with your mother. You can come back and talk about that if you want to." I went back. I wanted this horrible episode of my life behind me, and I didn't like the way I felt about my mother. The next session, I came away with two insights: one, the therapist thought I was afraid of my mother and two, she pointed out that I was lucky my mother was going to Florida for the winter.

Afraid of my mother? I decided to go tell her what was bothering me, which was what had happened, from my point of view, twenty-five years ago. I went in, sat down, and tried my best to tell what really happened. I think she thought I was crazy when I started to talk about what happened so long ago. I told her about the vet and how I had lost him. But when I tried to tell about being committed, she interrupted me.

"Lisa, you are blaming everyone else!" she said.

I stopped and thought about what I had just said. She was right.

"Yeah, it does sound like that doesn't it," I said. That was not what I wanted to say. But why did it come out that way? Puzzled, I left. I needed more time to think how to explain what happened. I was glad she was leaving for the winter. It gave me more time. I needed better communication skills.

I wanted to put this ordeal behind me in the worst way. I talked about it a lot. I wasn't going to shut down as I did twenty-five years ago. I was going to get this out of my system. I talked about it with old friends and new ones. It was fascinating as each person gave me a new piece of insight. I told my new pastor about what had happened at the old church and all that transpired, and he patiently listened, and at the end, his only comment was, "It's the people you are around." That was a dose of cold water. I was horrified.

"Those are all the people I grew up with!" I responded. It took me awhile to wrap my brain around that one.

The people who supposedly loved me the most, hurt me the deepest. How could this happen? It was not the people across the world or even across the room. It was not the person who looked differently, acted differently, thought differently or even worshiped differently. Those people were never let in close enough to hurt me. It was the people who I loved, who hurt me the most. The others were just on the surface, and they couldn't hurt as deep. It was easy to blame someone else, but it took courage to look within, to face personal pain, and to solve buried issues.

The more friends I connected with, the more healing I gained. One friend's comment, after hearing what my mother had done, was "Trophy child!"

"What's that?" I asked.

She proceeded to say, "That's the child that is held so special by the parent that they want everything for them. They want them to have it all. They put them in every sport or program, and they try to protect them from the world." I thought about it as an adult, looking back on when I was a child. I called it "surviving the perfect syndrome." I tried to put in practice the criticism that would make me perfect in her eyes.

I think the biggest fear as a child is the fear of disappointing. I think that is the fear of my mother the therapist was talking about---that I might disappoint her. I tried to be perfect. I graduated high school third out of a graduating class of 301. I graduated from college Cum Laude, just points from Magna Cum Laude. I tried to do everything I thought she expected.

She taught me, "You can do anything you set your mind to." And "Where there's a will there's a way." I had achieved countless successes with her advice but trying to be perfect was an impossible achievement.

I remembered my mom getting mad with me only once as a child, and that was when I wouldn't let go of her arm when she was trying her best to leave me the first day of first grade and get to work on time. She gave me the ugliest look in the world, as she jerked her arm away, and left. After that, I don't ever remember her getting mad with me, and I trusted her more than anything else in the world. That unquestioned trust was the reason I found myself committed. As a child, moms know best. But I was an adult. And I trusted that if she said she was picking me up the next morning after I escaped the lockup, she would be there. What a rude awakening her betrayal was. I should never have been there in the first place.

Just think, moms are the most powerful people in the world, in a kid's world anyway. Moms have power over molding adults. Dads too.

While I was in my childhood looking for answers, I thought about my relationship with my dad. I thought about two wonderful childhood memories that both happened in the first grade. He brought our new dachshund puppy to my class, and I was so thrilled to show all my classmates my new puppy and my dad who was so cool. Another time, he drove me to the new construction site of a shopping center in the neighboring town. It was the longest building I had ever seen, but the best part of the occasion was that it was just my dad and me and no one else. I felt so special.

There were memories that were not so great. I remembered the first time I helped my friends who were boarding and training my horse and getting my horse to a show. I spent the night with them and spent all day washing horses and tack, then loading and unloading. At the horse show that night, I ran in great excitement up to my parents to tell them of my accomplishments. In the middle of my conversation, my dad, the dentist, quite rudely interrupted, pulled my lip back and said, "Have you brushed your teeth today?" I couldn't believe it. Didn't he hear a word of my accomplishments?

I remembered helping my dad in his garden for hours upon hours in the summer and asking him if we could get an ice cream cone, just he and I. Rarely did he answer me, and I couldn't understand why I wasn't worth as much as a fifteen-cent ice cream cone for all the help I gave him.

The next memory, I was of driving age and allowed to use a family car. In appreciation, I spent all afternoon washing the car, inside and out and couldn't wait for my dad to see it. He came home in an angry fuss. "Who left the hose out?" he yelled. I was too shaken to ask him if he liked the car wash. I guess there was nothing to be heard if I didn't talk back. When my dad's anger came out, I kept my mouth shut. I wasn't learning how to communicate, I was learning to turn within myself for comfort. Suppression?

No wonder I put up with my husband's verbal abuse for so long. I had been conditioned for it as a child. My mom was the calm one and tried to buffer my dad's anger, but abuse shouldn't happen in a child's life no matter how you cut it.

I had three brothers, and I would watch my dad play football and roughhouse with the boys. Every time I walked on the field, the playing would all stop. But I was small, like age four. I could remember thinking one day as I sat on the porch, if I were a boy, my dad would love me too. At that point, a tomboy was born. Little did I know, he probably loved me just the same, but didn't remember ever hearing from my dad, "I love you."

But eventually, good memories started to come back. I used to sometimes sit in the bathroom with my dad when he shaved. As he looked in the mirror, he talked about integrity. Doing the right thing, even when no one was looking, so he could look himself in the mirror, he would say.

Dad was an avid golfer. His favorite joke was that a man came home late one evening and told his wife he had spent all afternoon at a hotel with a blonde bombshell. The wife scoffed at the thought and said, "Yeah right. You played 36 holes."

My dad had a beautiful voice, and he sang in the church choir. I could still hear him sing his favorite hymns: 'How Great Thou Art, The Old Rugged Cross, and Mother Macrae.' His voice allowed him to be the announcer at the high school basketball and football games. It allowed me to get into the games for free.

Thanks to my dentist dad, I have no cavities in my teeth. He came to my elementary school classes and taught my classmates how to properly brush and floss their teeth.

Although his dad, Pa, drank, my dad rarely drank more than an occasional glass of wine, but golf was his drug. He would come tearing in the driveway after work, change his clothes, and then go tearing out. My mom entertained us with making a joke of staying out of his way. He justified spending money on golf by saying it was a whole lot cheaper than alcohol. That's true.

He drove a car and played golf like a man on steroids. Yet, he was. Around the time I was in primary grades, he and Mom discovered he had a brain tumor that destroyed part of his pituitary gland, the gland that controls all other glands. The tumor was irradiated, which stopped the growth, but the treatment was to be on cortisone, a steroid, for the rest of his life. I wonder if being on steroids could explain his short fuse to anger?

Whatever was in front of him, he had to pass it, whether on the road or on the golf course. I tried one day, while playing golf with him, to explain that golf was called "a round," you just get in and play around the course in the groove with everyone else. He said he understood what I was saying, as we played through whoever was in front of us. Maybe he did understand it, but he just couldn't do it. Maybe steroids were just 'go juice'. We would hit extra golf balls sometimes and it was my job to get low in the golf cart and lean out and scoop them up as he sped by.

"Dad, think you could stop?" I asked. Not in his DNA. But it was a fun game. One day, I leaned way out to the right to pick up the last ball and as soon as I did, he took a sharp turn to the left and it was all I could do to keep from rolling out on my head.

"DAD!" I exclaimed.

"Oh sorry," he said, as he never took his foot off the gas.

He drove a car the same way. Passed everything on the road and slung his passengers around curves. I guess I didn't need to experience right to learn to do right. He gave me the best lesson on how to haul horses. I drive quite smoothly. Horses must stand up, at least we got to sit down.

Before he died, I learned the story of why he drove as he did. He was drafted into the Army near the end of WWII and was stationed in the Philippines. He was in the infantry, and somehow, he was selected to help the medics in the hospital as an ambulance driver. They gave him a quick lesson in driving, wrote him out a license and told him to drive very erratically to make his vehicle difficult to target. I guess old habits die hard. He bragged he was a great driver because he never had an accident. That's true, but he could scare you to death if you were not accustomed to his driving.

"You must be the bravest woman in the world to ride with him!" said one of his fellow Lions Club members to my mom, after riding with him down the mountain to Mt. Airy and back. She was greatly amused.

He paid his way through college. He went to dental school on the GI bill, worked in the cafeteria, and General Mills Foods gave him a stipend. When possible, he made sure General Mills made the cereals we bought.

He was one of a handful of dentists in town. It wasn't always a pleasant experience to see him, and many were a little scared to go as he was such a perfectionist. He could become very aggravated while you were in his chair. People were afraid to go to him, but more afraid not to because his work was nothing short of a masterpiece. He made his dentures imperfect like real teeth, and his patients were thrilled that no one could tell their teeth were false. My first cousin loved to tell about his new dentist marveling over a filling my dad had put in, which had held in his tooth for more than forty years and was still holding.

He worked until he had a stroke that affected his left arm, leg, and mouth. He went to rehab therapy like his golf game, a man on a mission. And it was his love for golf that pulled him through. He was determined to get out and play again. And he did. A year later, his doctor discovered the tumor came back and he needed surgery. On a Friday, the surgeon cut a hole in his skull at his right temple, removed the tumor, and put the skull piece back. He was out on Monday. We teased that he had drive-by brain surgery. He eventually got back out on the golf course. A year later, the tumor came back. The surgeon repeated the operation, and this time left out the skull piece which was riddled with cancer. My dad eventually got back on the golf course with a batter's hat to protect his head.

A year later, the tumor came back as we could tell with the loss of his motor skills and some of his thought process. He got in bad shape very quickly, and we took him back and asked the surgeon if he could get him back on the golf course.

"I didn't think I could get him there the first time," the surgeon replied.

Dad had slipped into what appeared to be a coma. It was a sobering experience to know there was nothing that could help. He went down pretty fast and didn't respond anymore. My dad left this world on his birthday.

Before he died, my husband and I went to visit him in the hospital. My mom was there sitting with him. When we got ready to leave, I sat on his bed up close to his head and leaned in.

"Dad, I'm going home. Give me a hug," I said. He didn't respond, and his right hand moved around his nose like he was swatting at a fly. I moved in a little closer.

"Dad, I'm going home. Give me a hug," I said louder. Lo and behold, he did it! Tom and Mom were both surprised. It felt great! One, he did it, and two, we never hugged. I sat up in awe.

"He did it!" I said with surprise.

That heartfelt hug gave me closure to my imperfect relationship with my dad. As we got up to leave, Tom stepped over to give Mom a hug and she abruptly stepped back and put her hands out to stop him.

"I'm ok, I'm ok," she said. My husband talked about her recoil several times over the years. That was the way the WWII generation in my family acted. You always showed strength, and never did you show vulnerability.

I did the same thing with my son, and this was one of the main things I worked on changing, to hug him as often as possible. That's pretty tough when he got to be a teenager, but I worked at it in any way.

He now likes a hug when he does something good, and he loves one when things don't work out so well. I think a hug is a great accomplishment. Now he likes a hug anytime. At my dad's funeral, I wanted to tell about that wonderful hug experience, but my mom said no. Again, I was silenced. Did that fall under keeping family secrets?

I waited until I was almost thirty-four years old before I ever got married, because I thought, after living with the craziness and hollering from my dad, maybe I didn't ever want to be married. I had heard "Little girls marry their fathers," meaning they marry someone like their dads. My dad was an adult child of an alcoholic, so was my husband and both were doctors. Since my mother was so h*llbent that "I needed a doctor," did I marry a doctor to make my mother happy? Good question. Another woman had trapped the man I had wanted.

Several months passed and, after having as little contact as I could with my mother, I decided to talk to her again and tell her my side of the story about being committed. This time, I did a better job with telling the facts and not sounding like I was blaming anyone. But what stood out in that confrontation was the end when I defended myself from the episode with the preacher.

"That disagreement was between the preacher and me, and you shouldn't have gotten in the middle of it in the first place. But the fact you took the preacher's side over your own daughter, frankly Mom, that broke my heart. You told me all my life that I was responsible for my own actions. So why was my brother not responsible for his anger and the preacher not responsible for his? If you ever hold me responsible for anyone else's anger again, I promise you, I will be mad." And this was most interesting. She looked down at the floor.

"Well, everyone has a right to be mad," she said.

That was the first time in MY life, that I had THE RIGHT to be mad! I realized I had lived my entire life under a double standard. The men always had a right to be mad, but I didn't, and more than half the time, I had been held responsible for their anger, which I had no control over. Yes, I could push their buttons, but I had to deal with my buttons, so guess what, guys who think you're God, you can deal with yours!

That was like what my husband had done to me for all these years. It was not my fault his first son from a previous marriage was a drug addict. But he did a lot of yelling and screaming at me because of it. Voicing frustration was one thing and making another person a whipping post was another.

I had years of anger pent up towards my husband and my mom. I think I finally just got tired of it. My mom wanted a relationship back, and I slowly started to soften. I still felt like she thought she was right about what she did twenty-five years ago. She had yet to see my side.

A few months later, I tried it one more time. I tried this time to convince her it wasn't crazy to pick up the hitchhiker. She started to argue her point and I finally gave up. She was NEVER going to hear me. I was finally ready to accept that fact. I gave up. I sat silent. She finally asked me what did I want to say.

"Mom, the hitchhiker looked like my younger brother. If he was broke down on the side of the road, wouldn't you want someone like me to pick him up?" By the look on her face, Bingo! I finally phrased it for her to understand.

"Mom, when I said I see pictures, I wasn't hallucinating like you thought, I think in pictures like most creative people do. You have seen me do this a hundred times. When you ask me to help you decorate a room, and I go in and look all around. I can picture the room perfectly as if it is already decorated, and then I describe it to you," I explained. The look on her face was one of surprise and amazement.

"Oh, I didn't know that," she said. She heard me.

The most ironic thing happened. A month later, while Mom was in Florida, a virus took almost all her hearing. Up to that point, she had dog hearing. Now I had to stand right in front of her and talk loud for her to hear me. I finally got her to hear to me...and now she can't hear me! I don't know. God works in mysterious ways. I sometimes wondered if God was teaching her a lesson. It took a year before her hearing was restored.

God does have a vengeance against wrong doing.

The same thing happened with her as it had with my dad. I began to start to remember the good stuff and the good times. I thought of who I had become because of my mother. I can cook, sew, shop, entertain, and display manners; be courteous, charming, trustworthy, bossy, sympathetic, compassionate and disciplined. I have always been slim, and I know that is from the care she took in making sure we had balanced meals and good eating habits. Maybe the most important lesson of all came later in life, not to let other people take over my world. My favorite, where there's a will, there's a way.

Mom had quit working after I was in first grade. When I was in about the fifth grade, Dad was diagnosed with his brain tumor. She thought it was a good idea to go back to work in case she needed to support her four children if something happened to Dad. So, she was hired by the high school to start a Nurses Aid and Intro to Health Care Class and kept our world organized. She hired a lady to help several hours a day with household chores and she stayed with us for fifteen years. We loved her as part of the family. When the local hospital was built, Mom turned the class into a Practical Nursing Program. One year into the program, Wytheville Community College picked up the program as dual credits could be applied to a RN degree. In time, Galax and Grayson County Schools combined with Carroll County High School into Twin County School of Practical Nursing. Mom was the Clinical Instructor and Director of the program. Countless students graduated board certified as LPNs. She could get things done without ever rocking the boat. Everyone loved her. This was all tied into the area hospital into which I was committed. She had silent power. No one questioned her judgement.

All power needs checks and balances.

I went to visit my mom and stepdad in Florida, I guess so I could show her the woman I had become and prove to her my way was right for me. I sat down at the table with her and my step dad and told him of one of our funny experiences. She remembered the restaurant of this incident, but she was more than confused about the location of the town. My stepdad tried to help straighten out her confusion. It appeared she had early Dementia or Alzheimer's. She got up to go to the bathroom and I looked over at my stepdad as he had given me a concerned look.

"I'm going to prove to you over the next couple of days, there's nothing wrong with her," I said. I recognized what it looks like when you have been robbed of all your power. I had thrown her out of my life earlier, my stepdad took her to Florida, away from her home, church, and family, and my sister-in-law took over running her kitchen.

For the next two days, Mom and I reminisced laughing at our countless prior shenanigans. She remembered stuff I even forgot. It became obvious there was nothing wrong with her. When she got back in town in the spring, I showed her Mark's trophy room and a large part was his big win at Roanoke. She hadn't been there because my stepdad had taken her back to the beach and I knew she wanted to be at that show. I rubbed it in she wasn't at the show, and reminded her when she agreed to marry, her own criteria was that the marriage was not to take away her family, home, or church.

"You know, Dad was a pain in the *ss, but you were a lot more fun," I said. She began to take her own life and power back. Her humor began to surface.

I can guarantee my mother's method of parenting was mostly handed down from her parents. You know a two-time WW soldier knows discipline. Discipline is an excellent thing but not to the point of suppression. Remember what the retired policeman said, "I guarantee, if the parents did it, the children do the same thing." So, I know exactly how she feels. I'm sure living under the magnifying glass of being a preacher's kid wasn't all fun and games either. Talk about surviving the perfect syndrome. But my life is my life, and I'm going to do with it as I please.

She gained her power back and asked me to be friends. I guess maybe the relationship as my mother is gone. Frankly, I like her a lot more as my friend. After more than half a century, I don't need a mother anymore. I don't think I needed to be mothered anymore after eighteen.

My grandmother Worrell laughingly told me I was an old maid at that age. What might I learn from visiting her memory?

24

My Grandmother Worrell

"Now there's true grit," my mom used to say about her mother-in-law. The definition came from the story about my grandmother taking a road trip in a Ford Model A to Baltimore, Maryland, in the late 1930s. All alone with her son, she traveled with no air conditioning, no four-lane highways, and no cell phone in case of a breakdown. The purpose of the trip was a treatment for her oldest son's polio. Rain, sleet, snow or sideways rain would not deter her from any possibility that might save him. She was a young mother, with an eighth-grade education, finding her way alone, over a three hundred and fifty-mile round trip. Sometimes, grit was not enough, because the oldest of her three sons, Marion Grey, died at the age of sixteen. She was the definition of a woman's true grit. There was nothing good mothers in my family wouldn't go through if we decided the effort would help our children.

Now, I'm sure that's why my mom was unstoppable. Come to think of it, as mothers, we were all unstoppable. She thought she was helping me. When I ask, her mature advice is very helpful. I'm giving advice the same for my own son.

My dad's parents were referred to as Ma and Pa Worrell. It reminds me of the TV version of Ma and Pa Kettle. Ma never had a 'real job,' but was a mom and housewife. Today, it is recognized as a job, back then, a way of life. While Pa worked, she did whatever she wanted, but she always had supper on the table when Pa came home. She always made us a chocolate pound cake with chocolate icing for our birthdays. She had one or two cakes made and kept in the freezer, so she could produce one in a hurry if needed. When she got up in years, she was going to quit making the cakes, and we would have to do without. We teased her and asked if she could make and freeze enough for after she was gone. She laughed at our ridiculous, heartfelt sympathy.

My grandparents lived two houses up from us, and Pa had Beagles in a pen in the bottom, a flat area, down the hill from the back of their house, alongside a nice rolling creek. My younger brother owns the home and property now, and he opens it up to park cars and RVs along the creek in the shade, during the Hillsville Labor Day Flea Market. The Beagles were Pa's rabbit hunting dogs. I never remember him hunting, but I guess he did.

Every year for April Fool's Day, we, the grandchildren, would take turns calling my grandparents and telling them the dogs were out, then run over to the window and watch them walk down the hill to check. Every year they fell for the same April Fool gag. We talked and laughed before we called, would this be the year we would get caught? They never seemed to catch on until they found the dogs safe in their pen. After Pa got sick, we still did it, and he would send Ma down there to check. Again, we laughed and so did they. A good, clean, practical joke always was worth a laugh.

One practical joke almost got out of hand. Between our houses, my dad had a quarter acre garden plot and Ma and Pa had one too. One year during cucumber harvest, my dad bought a green zucchini which none of us had seen before. It was two or three times the size of a cucumber but looked just like one. He placed it in Ma's cucumber patch without her knowledge. She found it with great surprise, jumped for joy at her supposedly prize cucumber, and the bragging rights began. I watched as my dad could barely keep the smirk off his face as he played along. She showed it to Dad, to Pa, and to Mom. She called her son, Joe, and she couldn't show it off enough, her prize cucumber. The biggest we had ever seen, although we knew it wasn't a cucumber.

The backfire came when Dad failed to recognize how far bragging rights would go. Pa's store was in the middle of town. They bragged to everyone. My dad's dental office was upstairs from the store, and when he came home for lunch, he was a little sheepish telling my mom that he knew someone would sometime recognize it for what it was. He didn't mean to embarrass them in front of everyone, just get a good laugh, which we all did the night before. Someone finally recognized what she had. I guess some practical jokes are destined to backfire. They continued to compete with their garden prizes, but that was the last big trick my dad played. We all felt bad about the embarrassment.

Just a few days ago, my mom said my younger brother, who owns and lives on Ma and Pa's property, is about to be a granddad and it is going to be really funny when his grandchild calls up and tells him his dogs are out.

"I just wrote that story! Do you remember the cucumber story? I asked.

"You know, I felt bad about that," she said.

"I wrote about that too!" I laughed.

This proves two things: There's nothing wrong with my mother's mind and craziness in our family is a hand-me-down.

Ma loved to think of things to do with us, her grandchildren. On nice summer days, we would walk up to visit her childhood house. Only the chimney was left standing. We would walk up the hill to the sight and along the way she would point out a birch tree and show me how to pull off a green twig, pull back the bark and suck on the twig. For a very short while, it would have a minty-like taste. "This was our chewing gum," she would say.

The location of this house was just down Beaver Dam Road, off Main Street on the northside of town. The area she knew as her home place was called Trot Town. Today, down the road and across the street, is the trailhead for the Beaver Dam Nature Trail, that winds its way behind the town of Hillsville and down to the Carroll Wellness Center.

She would call up sometime and say, "Let's go to Trot Town," and I knew she was ready for a walk.

"Ma, why do they call this Trot Town?" I asked her one day.

"Cause...it's just a trot from town!" she said.

Don't you just love the simplicity of those days?

My first cousin and I were riding in the back seat of her Chevrolet Caprice. In those days, cars were either custom or deluxe. This one was gold with a black vinyl top. She asked where we wanted to go.

"Tastee Freeze, Tastee Freeze!" we said with excitement and exuberance!

She wanted to go the Mountain Top Restaurant in Fancy Gap, which is now an antique and garden shop. She tried to talk us into her choice. She asked us again and again.

"Tastee Freeze, Tastee Freeze!" we sang. I'm sure we had ice cream on our minds.

She got aggravated with us because we didn't want to go where she wanted and gritted her teeth.

"You....you.... little...little.........SH**ASSES!" she snapped.

My cousin and I knew we were in big trouble and our heads spun around towards each other, our eyes were as big as saucers while our mouths dropped open. In just a few more seconds, we began to snigger we had just been called sh**asses by our grandmother. In about another half a minute, our giggling got the best of her and she started laughing with us. Best lesson I think I ever learned: how to cuss and laugh at yourself, all demonstrated in less than five minutes! We ended up at the Tasty Freeze!

Pa was an alcoholic, or maybe I should say, he drank. I never saw his bad side, I was so young. He ran the local Auto and Electric Supply and serviced what he sold, TVs and appliances. Remember when TVs could be repaired instead of just thrown away when they quit working? Before that, he ran a grocery store in the coal fields of West Virginia. He must not have drunk much, because he always supported his family.

Pa smoked Camel cigarettes for years, and finally, he had to undergo lung cancer surgery. The surgeon removed a lung and a half. Pa gave up smoking the unfiltered Camel cigarettes to the filtered Doral. Being stubborn runs deep.

Ma teased me when I turned eighteen that I was an old maid. She had gotten married at seventeen. She gave me a wedding band my dad had made her in dental school out of twenty-four karat gold. He used gold for fillings, and later silver. I kept the ring until I married sixteen years later and gave it to my husband on our wedding day. She never lived to see that day. The other thing she saved for me was the front page of a 1912 Roanoke Times announcing the shootout at the Courthouse, located in the middle of town. The story was getting nationwide attention, until the sinking of the Titanic overshadowed the event. The entire debacle started with an argument over a girl at a church picnic, caused a shootout in the courtroom, and ended with a nationwide manhunt and jail time. Our town was famous for a few days.

I helped the best I could when Ma got wheelchair bound. She weighed one hundred and eighty-five pounds and her legs just couldn't hold her up anymore. She could get up on her own from the wheelchair to the car, to the couch, or to the toilet. Her effort helped a lot.

I remember one day taking her to her doctor in Winston. After the appointment, she wanted to go to her favorite cafeteria for lunch. I weigh less than one hundred and twenty pounds, so pushing her up an incline or lifting her up on a curb was a job. I had done just that and was standing in front of the doors of the restaurant. I couldn't believe how many people walked in front of us. No one offered to hold the door open, or even slowed down enough so I could ask. It would have been easier if the door pushed, but it pulled open, which meant I had to get in front, pull the door open and while holding and pulling the loaded wheelchair. I struggled and got the job done, but I was so annoyed with the other patrons. Same thing on the way out. Once outside, a very nice lady walked up and asked if she could stand with my grandmother while I went to get the car. I was so thankful! She explained her late husband had been in a wheelchair and she understood the inconvenience. It was a great help an angel showed up. She stood alongside Ma who sat holding a piece of chocolate cheesecake she had bought, along with my lunch, as a gift for my efforts.

Ma got to the point of needing someone to stay with her at night. I volunteered to sleep in a bedroom above her room while I worked during the day. It went ok for a while, until I woke up to a thump. I ran downstairs and discovered she had fallen while trying to get in her wheelchair to go to the bathroom. I tried, but there was no way I could pick her up off the floor. There wasn't enough muscle tone in her arms for her to help me pick her up. I woke up the neighbor next door as she had instructed and together, we got her back into bed. It happened several more times and I begged Ma to call me before she tried. I found myself up most all night and working all day. She was constantly trying to go to the bathroom. I couldn't keep up the pace. I begged her to hire someone. I knew she could, she just wouldn't. I quit staying with her and then she hired someone. A stomach aneurysm was the reason she was getting up so many times a night. The doctors didn't think she would survive the surgery to fix it.

When it was apparent she was getting to her last days, and she refused to go to the hospital. She wanted to stay home. We let her do what she wanted. She was making sure her property and money was going to her last son, and six grandchildren, not to the hospital or a nursing home. She spoke to us until just a few hours before she died. Gritty to the end. She died on her favorite couch.

When my time comes, I intend to die on my terms and not under treatment that I don't want, because somebody else thinks it's better for me. I will die from the same disease. It is called "chronic stubbornism!" Apparently, it runs in the family. My plan is to go and go and go and one day, not wake up. We'll see.

Unfortunately, we don't get to plan who we are born to or how we get to go out. Everything else in between is optional. My boss used to say, "You don't HAVE to do anything, but DIE! I have found great power in that statement. Life is "butt" a choice. Sometimes it takes a sheer stubborn attitude to do what one feels is right.

It would have saved a lot of wear and tear on me had my grandmother's communication skills been a little better. The following example shows a backward-looking statement and the second a forward-looking statement. When I was about to be committed, instead of saying, "Where's Lisa, where's Lisa! She took all the handles off my cabinets!" Had she said, "Where's Lisa, where's Lisa! She promised to paint my cabinets!" Mom would have insisted I go to my grandmother's because I had made a promise. All I wanted to do anyway was work and be productive. Maybe my grandmother would have done me a great favor and locked me in her house until I finished, instead of helping to lock me in that d*mned hospital. I'm sure we would have had a lot more fun, and without a doubt, she would have bought me an ice cream cone at the Tastee Freeze for NOT being a SH**ASS!

I can't go back, only forward, but looking back on how I could change situations in the future is worth my reflecting time. It does pay to learn positive and forward-thinking communication skills.

I wish my husband could. Is he such a bad man? And what makes him like he is?

25

My Husband

I wish I could say once I realized the marital problems were half my fault and my husband were working with a marriage counselor, our marriage problems would end, but it wasn't quite that easy. Both were a significant milestone, but twenty years of a bumpy marriage didn't stop overnight. I hated turning into a roaring lion, but I had tried every other thing I knew. I was determined to make the remaining time at home for my son, and me, peaceful.

If you have ever tried to make a point with an addict or recovering addict, it is an exhausting experience. Or is it just men who don't know what "no" means? I would compare it to a game in the amusement park called Whack a Mole. When the mole pops its head up through one hole, you try to hit the mole on the head with a padded club. Usually, before you can, it disappears and pops its head out of another hole. And the game keeps going. It is very fast moving. When talking to an addict, the subject is here, then there, then here, then there. Blame here, blame there, blame everywhere. The sane person sees the lunacy in the conversation and gives up. I gave up because I thought the game was insane.

After losing my horse, my church, my mother, maybe my marriage and close friend...you wanna FIGHT? Ok, I'll fight. The first time I decided I was going to win the game of Whack a Mole, I had enough fight and anger in me to take on my husband plus an army. I was ready. Whatever subject he picked, I went there. Here, there, here, there. Finally, he repeated the exact same thing he had just said.

"Do you realize you are just repeating yourself?" I said.

Suddenly, he stopped and looked like he had no idea of what he was even saying. With a confused look on his face, he stood silent. I couldn't believe it. I had just won my first game of Whack a Mole!" I always saw the fighting as useless. I hoped he would too.

The only time we went anywhere together was when we followed our son's band to the high school football games. We were leaving one afternoon at 4 and I came in at that time instead of 3:30, as I told him I would. We got in the car and I was excited about going to the game. In the first three minutes, he harshly scolded me for not being home on time. He should have known better. The lion awoke!

I roared back, "YOU NEVER ASKED ME WHAT HAPPENED OR WHY I WAS LATE! DID A HORSE GET OUT, DID THE TRACTOR BREAKDOWN, DID I HAVE A FLAT TIRE? I AM TIRED OF YOU ATTACKING ME...." You get the picture. Our son wasn't around to hear the fight. I saw no need to hold back or freeze. Wasn't long before my husband wished he hadn't opened his mouth. Again, I won. Problem was, I didn't like to fight, so it didn't feel much like winning. But I had every right to defend myself. I just wanted his attacking to stop.

I didn't control what he did, I controlled what I did, and I gave him consequences for his actions. I used my anger as that consequence. Just like his kids used the wear down tactic and just like he used his anger to try to get his way with me. If he gave me a reason, I bit his head off. I wanted peace and I wanted peace in this household. I had heard enough.

I took my freedom back and went wherever I wanted. If I wanted to go to out of town, I went. If I wanted to go with a friend somewhere, I went. He wanted to know why we weren't going anywhere together.

"Because wherever I have ever gone with you, you always pick a fight. So, I'm not going with you anymore because I don't want to fight! I deserve to be happy, and I want to live in peace," I said.

I went wherever I could go on Saturdays to stay away from a fight and enjoy myself. I loved listening to my selections of music as I drove along. He finally convinced me to let him go along on a shopping trip less than an hour away.

"This is going to be a day of peace, listening to music, shopping in the mall, just a restful day. If you don't fight with me, you can go," I said.

He agreed. We were about twenty minutes from home, he wanted me to talk about stocks.

"I don't want to talk about stocks today. We'll do that another time," I said.

"Well, I DO want to talk about stocks!" he demanded.

"I don't want to talk about stocks," I repeated calmly.

"Well, I do!" he again demanded.

So, he started talking about stocks. When I didn't engage in the conversation, he got angry with me. I thought to myself, well, dealing with a civilized person, communication and accountability should work, but obviously, this was not civilized if he refused my request. My next three choices were fight, flight or freeze. Freezing or staying silent didn't work. Flight was not an option because we were going 70 MPH and I was not stepping out of the car. That left fight...which I hated to do. He demanded again we talk about stocks and I responded with an explosion that filled the inside of the car.

"You can be so sweet, or you can be the biggest b..." he said.

"SO, **DON'T**, STRIKE A MATCH!" I snapped.

It took fifty-three years to burn up my fuse, I didn't plan on growing another one! He refused to respect my wishes. I decided to give him consequences for his actions. It seemed to work.

Just like the wall plaques that say, "If Mama's not happy, nobody's happy." He began to learn it was not a good idea to make me angry or what I call "the red-hot poker treatment," prodding me until I got angry. I never raised my voice unless provoked. In fact, in twenty years, I have never called him a derogatory name. He can't say the same thing. I noticed he began to tiptoe around me.

"I have learned not to say this, or do that," he said. I felt like I was training him like a horse. I have trained a thousand-pound stud, a hundred and seventy-pound stud shouldn't be that much of a challenge. Thank God he was learning. But several days when I came in, he looked a little afraid he might wake the sleeping lion. He didn't like being screamed at any more than I liked doing it, but I had weathered his verbal abuse for years. He knew I had a house to go to and that he might lose half of everything he had. Divorce had come up in a discussion and I always knew I didn't have to walk away penniless, I didn't want to fight. He began to think before he spoke. After several days, I couldn't take him looking like he was living in fear. No one needs to live like that.

"Ok, I'll make a deal with you. I just want two things. If you give me those, I will be perfectly satisfied. I won't ask for a divorce, I won't take your house, and I won't take your money," I said.

"What are the two things?" He asked.

"I want peace, and I want kindness," I replied.

"That's it, that's all?" he said.

"That's it, that's all I want," I replied.

"Ok." He agreed.

For all the years we had lived together, I explained to him that he rarely gave me my space. He seemed to follow me to whatever room I went. Now I would go into the bedroom and read, and he learned to give me space. I would get up for quiet time with my coffee in the morning, and he learned not to be under my feet in the kitchen, or turn on the TV, and disrupt the quiet. I think having some time of quiet solitude in our home was not too much to ask. He knew better than to provoke a fight. But he came in the bedroom while I was reading one day.

"What were the two things you wanted? I can't remember," he said.

"Are you kidding me?" I said. I couldn't believe it.

"No, what were they again?" he said.

"Peace and kindness," I replied.

He went out mumbling to himself. In a few minutes, he came back.

"I better write that down," he said.

I thought, "ARE YOU KIDDING ME?"

He got out a piece of paper and pen.

"Ok...peace and... what was the other one?" he asked.

"KINDNESS," I snapped.

He wrote it down, mumbling peace and kindness, peace and kindness on his way out the door. I thought, "Oh God! This is never going to work."

For the next several days, he gave me peace. It was nice. I had my quiet time in the morning, I had quiet reading time and the tension seemed to lift. One day he walked up to me.

"Well, I've been trying to give you peace and kindness, how am I doing?" he asked.

"You're doing good," I said with a smile.

He looked pleased with himself and walked into another room. We went on a little thirty-minute short trip, and it was quiet. Not much talk, but what little there was, it was pleasant and best of all, no arguing. I was listening to music like I did all the time when he wasn't with me.

"I've been trying to give you peace, am I doing ok?" he said.

"Yes, you are doing good, thank you," I replied, and smiled.

After years and years of being fussed at almost every day when I walked in the door, and it stopped, I felt like I had been leaning into a fifty mile an hour wind and suddenly the wind quit. I didn't fall on my face, but it took a little time to equilibrate. This adjustment, I was happy to make. I slowly acclimated to being comfortable in our home. It was about time.

This was what I really thought of my husband, Tom. He came from almost abject poverty to put himself through medical school and became a doctor. I admired that and always had. He didn't grow up with a silver spoon in his mouth, and he earned everything he had. I respected that. His accomplishments came from a less than perfect childhood. My husband, Tom, was to be admired.

Tom showed me the house he grew up in, and it would fit in less than two rooms in our current residence. He liked to drive by his house every time we went to Columbia, South Carolina. He lived there with his mother, father, grandmother, and sister. All the years my husband grew up were riddled with his father's drinking, disappearing, employment, unemployment, disappearing, and drinking and the cycle went on and on. My grandfather, Pa, was much more functional than that.

His grandmother worked in the school cafeteria while his mother learned to type and had a couple of secretarial jobs. Both helped to make ends meet. His mother divorced his dad twice and married him three times, hoping each time would be different. There was a five-year stent when things were relatively quiet, and they did things as a family. There was a period, after his parent's first divorce, he and his sister had to go live with an aunt because his mother was hospitalized with major depression. He never got over not being able to take his adopted dog with him and remembered driving off watching his dog upset being left behind. The guilt he must have felt for abandoning his dog. For all our marriage, any dog that wandered in wanting a home, Tom gave it one.

The most significant impact on his life started during the time his mother was hospitalized. His grandfather picked him up and took him to stay with him and his grandmother in Waynesville, North Carolina, starting when Tom was twelve years old. His grandfather had been very successful in the lumber business, and they lived in a lovely house with a maid and manservant. His grandparents were known to their family as Daddy Whitty and Mama Whitty.

Mama Whitty made sure she was always put together 'just so' whenever she went out or anyone came to visit. She was two or three years late at collecting Social Security because she was too stubborn to tell her age, and no one knew how old she was. It looked to me she had way more vanity than compassion. Maybe that explained why Tom's dad, Mama Whitty's son, drank so much. Was he nurtured?

Tom was most impressed with his grandfather's 1951 green Buick Super. With Daddy Whitty's business success, every day he gave Tom a dollar. With that dollar, he went to the movies, bought a five-cent green sucker, a model airplane to put together, a coke cola at the drug store, and read a comic book off the rack. After reading the comic book, he would place it back on the stand, and the guy behind the counter never said a word. When he went out to eat with his grandfather, sometimes he couldn't decide between a hamburger or a hotdog, and his Daddy Whitty told him to get both. In pictures I saw of him during that time, he needed both. Daddy Whitty wanted to be sure Tom had enough to eat.

Spending three wonderful summers with his grandfather, Tom decided he wanted to be like him, drive a big fine car, own a lovely house, make plenty of money to spend and not be poor anymore. So, Tom decided then he wanted to become a doctor, someone people would respect.

His grandfather was the positive influence on his life. Kindness and generosity had great power.

Tom worked almost three years delivering newspapers from his bicycle every morning before school. It paid $100 a month, and college tuition was $300 a semester. His mother helped also. When he got into medical school, a doctor in town helped him with expenses as he had helped other medical students. He instructed Tom not to get married until he graduated, because the doctor had gotten married before finishing and he knew how hard it was. The doctor helped for two years, and during one of their periodic visits, Tom informed him he was engaged. The doctor was annoyed and wasn't going to help him anymore, and Tom said that was ok. On his way out the door, the doctor's wife whispered, "Don't you worry, if you need anything, I will help you." Tom married his new wife who was a school teacher, and they made it on their own.

After graduating from Med school, he chose to join the Navy. If he hadn't volunteered, the Army would have drafted him as a doctor to help during the Vietnam War. He volunteered for sea duty and served two years in the Navy on a submarine tender as the ship's doctor. After discharge, he wanted to go into residency for general surgery, but to get in, he had to wait a year. He moved to Gastonia, North Carolina and worked in the emergency room. In a year, he moved his family to Augusta, Georgia to be a resident in general surgery. It worked him to death by being on call every other night and never seeing his family. He quit the residency because the quality of life was awful.

He moved back to Columbia, opened his own office in family practice with a doctor friend, saw patients in the morning and did hospital rounds in the afternoon. An office visit had gone up to $5 from $3. Every third day, he was on call and sometimes was called out of bed several times a night. The doctor a few blocks away committed suicide, and Tom and his partner were overwhelmed with the patient load. He had been feeling bad during this time and discovered he had diabetes. After a couple of years of an impossible workload, diabetes was taking its toll, he self-prescribed an oral dose Talwin, non-addictive opioid, to relieve the pain of headaches. He didn't feel like under the circumstances, that he could remain in family practice, so he took his family back to Charleston to do a residency in pathology. With two small children, his wife had to go back to work to make ends meet again. He worked forty hours at the VA hospital with not much pay and moonlighted on the weekends with twenty-four-hour shifts in the emergency room to help with living expenses. Each time he moved to be near his job or school, he bought and sold the houses that he lived in for a profit. He still wasn't making much money until finally he was hired for the pathology position in Galax, Virginia.

While setting up his own corporation and meeting with lawyers, the headaches came back. He had a small vial of Talwin from his family practice bag and this time he injected a small dose. The headache was fixed immediately. More headaches, more Talwin. After about three weeks, he realized without it, he felt awful. He knew he was addicted. Doctors had parties, served alcohol, and life was good before managed care came into communities. Tom and his wife socialized and had toddies for years. The Talwin continued. His wife began to find boxes of empty vials and suggested he do something. He agreed but never went for help. Each order he intended it to be the last. Finally, one doctor in town shot himself after his drug abuse and his anger ruined his practice. No one wanted to go see him. Watching this downfall, Tom and his wife decided it was time to do something about his drug addiction.

Tom volunteered to go into rehab and the hospital promised to hold his job. He never lost his license because he came forward on his own. The hospital hired a pathologist during his time away and reviewed his work from the previous year to see if it had affected his work. His work was good. He was in treatment for eight to ten weeks when an associate informed him that his wife was diagnosed with colon cancer and her liver was ninety-five percent consumed with cancer. Drug rehab let him have time off. At this time, his children were of college age. She died three weeks after her cancer was first discovered. He went back to treatment and they helped him deal with his grief. He returned to his job clean of all alcohol and drugs and remained so ever since. While on vacation with his daughter, he received a midnight call that his house had burned completely to the ground. He didn't tell his daughter until the next day. There was nothing to be done, so they went sailing. He unsuccessfully remarried, and the divorce was not pretty.

All these things happened before I ever met my husband. When we married, I had met his daughter, and she came to our wedding. Our relationship grew. I had never met his adult son and never dreamed their relationship would have any effect on my life. As far as I was concerned, his kids were grown and gone. However, the dysfunctional relationship between the drug-addicted son and my husband created chaos I never even imagined. What drugs and alcohol could do to family life was nothing short of abusive. My husband had no role model to go by, to have any parenting skills, although he tried his best. I had the knowledge to teach children discipline and run an organized household but rarely gained the respect to carry it out no matter how hard I tried. You give me an addict, and I will give you an enabler. It took me sixteen years to convince my husband to stop running around with a safety net and let his adult son live the consequences of his actions.

Had the problem with his son been my responsibility, I would not have fed into his son's immediate gratification or given him a handout to keep him from falling on his face. There was a difference in trying to control what someone else does as opposed to giving consequences for their actions. And that was the basis for most of our arguments. I tried to stop what had gone wrong for many years. As I saw it, his adult son was no longer a child and needed to be responsible for himself.

While the prior preacher and I were still on good terms, I asked for his help to convince my husband to stop enabling his adult son. Together, the three of us came up with a plan to cut the apron strings. Our plan achieved Tom's adult son signing himself into a drug rehab program. His son came out with a new plan on life and I eventually tried my hand in helping my stepson. I had gotten tired of his excuses not applying for jobs because he couldn't get around. I had lucked into a great deal on a brand-new gasoline scooter to get around on horse show grounds. It weighed three hundred pounds which was too heavy for me to load in my horse trailer. So, I told my stepson if he would come over and learn to ride it, I would give it to him. He was doing good, but near the end of his maiden voyage, he crashed into a roadside rock formation, ruptured his spleen and cracked two vertebras. The 'Evil Step Mother' almost killed him! That was the first and last time I would help an adult son more than just moral support and solicited advice! The accident also educated Tom and myself that rehab had got him off street drugs and put him on the government drug, Methadone. The adult son was happy still being on a drug until the money, Tom promised him, ran out. The drug addicted adult weaned himself off Methadone because he couldn't afford the habit anymore. No more enabling WORKED!

Tom's adult son now supports himself, and he and my husband have an adult friendship. Without the enabling, his son has made a life for himself. I wish I had been more skillful in supporting them both and I really wish I hadn't helped. Positive communications skills and accountability, being responsible for oneself, would have made life easier for all involved.

When I finally got Tom to give me peace and kindness, a new and better relationship grew. Both of us like the peace. We both choose our words more carefully to be kinder to the other. He has started a new tradition to serve me breakfast in bed on Sundays. I compliment him on his meals and thank him for doing the shopping. We both are much kinder to each other. He has been supportive of my new business venture. I try to make our life enjoyable, pleasurable, and pick places to go for fun.

One morning, Tom told me of a dream that left him feeling very upset. I asked him to share it.

"There was this big bulldozer that was destroying our home and I was mad at my mother because she wouldn't do anything to stop it," he said.

I thought about it a minute.

"Don't you think the bulldozer was your father's drinking problem that was destroying your home life? I can understand you being mad at your mother for not stopping it," I asked.

"That's good, and I think you're right," he said.

He felt the same as I felt, and our son felt, wishing mom would put a stop to dad's abusive behavior. Do women realize how important a job it is to protect the children? Do men? I always felt like something Tom's mother did was the root of how he treated me, so I asked him what made him feel so insecure about his childhood experience.

"I'll tell you exactly...when I was three and my dad was drinking, my mom was a nervous kind of woman. If something happened to her, what would happen to me?" he said.

He was afraid she would abandon him. She became very depressed about ten years later, and, because of her depression, he lost his little dog he loved so much. She must have felt guilty for abandoning him. He added that his pathology instructor criticized continuously, not just him, but all his students. The instructor would set him up to present in front of a large group, interrupt him, and cut him down in front of everyone.

People can be cruel, and I'm not sure they even realize it. How a person can carry fear and anger through most of a lifetime is now understandable. I carried anger, and so did my husband. Words can lift, and words can destroy.

Both of us were very defensive when criticized. I had been working hard at changing my tune, and I worked hard at trying to convince my husband to choose his words carefully. Doing the same thing over and over again for years and years is an unbelievably hard habit to break. Positive communication skills solve a lot of problems, and so does the ability to set boundaries. I wish we would have just merely set up a "timeout" rule at the beginning of the marriage. Either one of us could call a timeout and arguments just stop until things cooled off. Neither one of us thinks at the speed of a computer. It takes a human mind time to process things.

No walk of life is immune to the effects of drugs and alcohol on family dysfunction and relationships. Even without impairment, many people lack parenting and relationship skills.

In one way, my husband and I were entirely opposites. Just like I've always heard, opposites attract. We pulled each other to the middle to find a parenting balance.

I was determined to find more balance in my life.

IX

A Team of Support on the Road to Peace

26

My New Church

After leaving the old church, I didn't want a new one. While chaperoning one of our son's band competitions, I overheard a parent excited about her new trumpet. I learned she played in church. I was interested to hear her perform and called her one Saturday and asked if she was playing the next day. I was in luck. I discussed it with my son who played the trumpet, and he wanted to hear her too. I woke him up on Sunday morning, so we could go on our planned adventure. I got ready and he never came down from his room upstairs.

I went up to my son's room and he was still in bed.

"Are you going with me today?" I asked.

He grunted.

"Son, you have seen what it looks like on a day when you don't get out of bed. This isn't one of them!" I said.

He flew out of bed! I couldn't help but laugh!

The trumpeter was worth the effort, and she invited my son to bring his guitar, practice with the youth praise band, and join the youth group meeting that same day. He already knew some of the boys who were there from his boy scout troop. He was excited to join his friends. It was a match for him from the start.

I went each Sunday and took my son to his new groups, but it was a while before I felt comfortable. An old friend suggested joining her in the choir.

"It is fun!" she promised!

At the time, **no** place in **my** life was fun. Joining the choir was something I always wanted to try, like my dad, but I had always been too shy. But this time, I was ready to give it a try to find some fun in this life.

I'll never forget the first practice. After the hurt from the previous church experience, I didn't know who to trust. As soon as I took a seat in the choir room, they handed me the book for the Christmas program. I have read music, but this had so many parts on one page, I had no idea what I was doing. A very nice lady sitting beside me marked the two lines I was supposed to sing out of many lines per page. Two lines here, two lines there, turn the page. I could barely keep up. At the end of practice, the choir director gave some directions.

"Say hi to Lisa and get her a robe. We're like the mafia. Once you get in, you can't get out!" she teased.

The hair stood up on the back of my neck, and it was **a miracle** I didn't bolt for the door! The fear of being trapped again was almost overwhelming! I could barely process they were kidding!

"No, no, no, no, no! Just let me see if I can do this first!" I stuttered. It was an amusing way of working through the issue of trust. I had a lot of work to do.

I got lucky when a music major took me under her wing and was very kind and encouraging. I was brave and tested telling the truth.

"I can read music, but my voice can't," I softly said. This time, telling the truth didn't get me in deeper trouble.

What would be the reaction if people knew my commitment story? I went out on a limb and told the truth to test the reaction with my new voice coach and girlfriend. She thought my experience was awful, but what a relief as I realized it didn't faze our friendship in the least. Why would it? It happened to me, not her. It didn't change the fun of our bond in the least. It took the longest time for me to realize, my past didn't matter. It was what I could do now that I or anyone cared about.

About a year later, she said, "I like when you sit beside me because if I go out on a limb, you go with me."

I thought, "Uh oh, I didn't know we were going out on a limb, but I trust you will never lead me astray." These encounters helped me restore my faith in trust.

Three years later, I can read music, but my voice can't. I can easily sing in harmony within the chord, but not necessarily the exact note if I'm left on my own. I can read that note is an E, and I can match the music major's voice beside of me. What we can do together is delightful. But I cannot produce what I read without hearing it. I have learned to sing my part with her help and a good ear. I can hear harmony and match vibration. I understand how Beethoven could still write music, by feeling vibration, after he went deaf. A church organ provides vibration for anyone to feel. Besides that, actual music can be heard and felt, but never seen, so maybe not being able to produce what I see is understandable. Now I know why some of the great voices started in church choir like Elvis and Whitney Houston. It's a great place to learn and practice performing.

Singing in the choir becomes a game to monkey hear, monkey do. On Sundays when we sing regular hymns, which a lot I didn't know, only the words are given and no music. I must think on my feet and do what I hear. Since my friend and I sing alto, so often my friend sings an echo, which repeats part of the stanza. If she does it, I follow, because I trust she is right. If I don't, she elbows me in the ribs. I have become the instruments she plays. On stage, my voice coach and I are on display happily working together with all the choir to create harmony for all to enjoy.

My experience with her is like sitting next to God. If I follow, all is good. If I don't, I experience vengeance. **I get it!** Oh God, I promise I will use my talent for the good! I'm not perfect, please, forgive me. I will do my best to create peace and harmony in your creation.

Without my voice coach, I would had given up a long time ago, because it was challenging for an old dog to learn a new trick. I so appreciated my girlfriend's lead, and I made sure we often shared kiddie cups of various flavors of frozen yogurt. I took her to the dinner theater to watch a musical. I couldn't thank her enough for her kindness. Kindness had great power.

The choir was an enjoyable experience. I had great fun, which was why I came in the first place. I loved being in the company of other artists. Watching the entire music production fall together was an exciting experience. We practiced for months to learn the music. The last week before our production of praise, we practiced every day in the sanctuary to get the sound right. The narrators and actors came into the mix, along with props set in place. On Wednesday, the orchestra, directed by my trumpet friend, came in to play. On Friday, we were joined by the violins and cello. We performed on Saturday and Sunday evenings, and both nights ended in a standing ovation.

One experience took me by surprise. While participating in the live performance, I got so caught up in the play that for a few minutes I left the stage without moving from my chair. I was unaware of all my surrounding except the drama unfolding in front of me. It was like I was a fly on the stable wall in Bethlehem seeing Mary and Joseph's baby for the first time. The real-life couple with their newborn baby, their loving gaze was not an act, and I realized with EVERY baby, there is HOPE for a BETTER WORLD. I came back to earth when the choir was called to sing.

It brought my own bundle of joy more into focus. Our child is a gift. So, for years, just like a present on Christmas, I have been opening him up to see what I get. A doctor, engineer, horseman, swimmer, the gift that keeps on giving, endless episodes to enjoy. He is planning for college and I'm still waiting to see what I get.

The same feeling came again during the first Easter production, and again, for a moment, I left the stage. It was when Judas betrayed Jesus with a kiss; the iciest, coldest chill I ever felt, ran up the back of my spine and when it got to the top, the hair stood up on the back of my neck. It was a chilling experience.

The next night, I noticed all the actors in the play had taken off their glasses and watches to stay true to the period of around 2000 years ago. The pastor was playing Judas, and I teased him if he saw well enough not to fall off the stage. Here is a perfect example of having to relearn to speak. I had the chilling experience the night before.

"Well, maybe it's ok if you do fall off the stage," I said to the pastor.

I was so caught up in the emotion of the drama, and I was truly mad with Judas, the pastor, for being the betrayer. My comment didn't make the pastor very happy. He was unaware of my experience, and my poor choice of words came as a shock to him. What I should have said was, "Your performance was so realistic, I got caught up in the drama." Much better. Or better yet, "You did a good job playing your part." It pays to learn positive communication skills.

I've spent years giving performances in horse competitions, so I have no problem being on stage. But to give a performance just for the appreciation of it, without being judged, is absolutely wonderful. What I like most about participating is working together for a common goal, harmony in numbers, not trying to win over someone else. Quite a bit different from horse shows.

Isn't it funny how things work? Reluctantly, leaving my childhood church helped guide me to this new one more suited for my family and me. I didn't ask or pray for a new church and it just has happened. That's how grace is. I remember hearing one preacher years ago, describe grace like this..."While traveling through the South, every time he orders eggs at breakfast, this somewhat creamy but gritty white stuff comes on his plate. He asks the waitress what is this and he didn't order it."

"Oh, honey, that's grits. You don't order grits. It just comes," she says.

So, his lesson for that day..."God's grace is like grits. You don't ask for it, it just comes."

So just like grits, I was served a new church.

My new Sunday School class has one of the best Bible teachers I've ever had. He's great at explaining the lessons. One Sunday, we studied the story in Genesis about Abraham's plan to sacrifice his son Isaac, and my teacher asked how was Abraham able to tie Isaac up. He was sure Isaac was in on Abraham's plan. I disagreed that Isaac knew because I had first-hand knowledge we sometimes trust our parents to a fault. Fortunately, God spoke to Abraham and stopped him. Was my mom not listening or was God's plan was just a little different for me?

I had heard these stories throughout my entire life, but now they were beginning to come to life. I never dreamed I would be experiencing them.

Twenty-five years ago, before I came home, I knew something was wrong and I prayed to God to help me. I headed home, played Good Samaritan on the way, helped my grandmother and soon found myself locked up in a mental hospital. The entire episode cost me two years of my life, all the money I had saved, the rental house I so loved, and the life I had carved out for myself.

"What in the heck was God thinking if this was the help he gave me?" I thought. For the next twenty-five years, I didn't bother to talk to God. I lived the story of Job. Like him, I was upset about losing everything I worked for and couldn't understand why God answered my prayers as he did. Was I being tested like Job?

During this time, my son was born. I had gotten over questioning God, but I wondered if there was a God. I believed the teachings of Christ were the best at civilizing people. They teach how to love one another and love thy neighbor as thyself. If peace is the goal, the

Golden Rule holds true: Do unto others as you would have them do unto you.

A local church marque makes a good point as it said: "We have 35 million laws trying to enforce ten commandments." People do make things complicated. Seems to me, life would be a lot easier if more time were spent trying to get **along**, instead of trying to get **ahead**.

I made sure in my son's early years he heard the stories of the Bible. A parent in my former church introduced us to the Montessori method of telling Bible stories. Godly play. I made small props of the places, and people out of wood and my mother joined in and taught, so my son and the other children could see and experience the stories. I was amazed the following year when we started to retell a story, my son popped up and exclaimed, "I've already heard this story!" He was about six. I had to keep making new props for more stories until his age of ten. Their favorite story was Noah's Ark, and the children sailed the ark and arranged the animals as if they were Noah. They experienced the stories as children; as adults, we sometimes live them. The Bible stories are universal and timeless; therefore, the Biblical people are not outdated, just their technology.

In Genesis, Jacob fell in love with Rachel and was tricked into marrying her older sister, Leah. My Sunday school teacher asked, "How did Rachel feel?" I will tell you...."She was HEARTBROKEN when her sister stole the man she wanted from her!" I know all about that story! I never dreamed I would experience the stories. The word of God is true.

I listened one day very intently when my teacher dissected a story in the Song of Solomon about a man praising the beauty and value of his wife. He described his love and her beauty in comparisons to his possessions and property. I realized how hard it was for men to put their feelings into words. Solomon was trying to say he valued her. I used this in reverse to try to get through to my husband. One day I watched him, as many times before, get on the floor with his dogs and talk sweetly to them, lay in the floor with them, pet them ever so gently and spoil them with treats.

"Can't you just treat me like one of your dogs?" I said.

He patted me on the head and next day he bought me my favorite treat of Peanut M&Ms. I couldn't help but chuckle! It was a start! And the 'good' idea came straight from the "Good Book" itself.

I had often heard people tell of their "Come to Jesus moment." At first, I thought, "Wonder what they have been smoking?" Sometimes I thought they sounded crazy, and finally I just thought it was nice and wondered if it was true and would it ever happen to me? Who would have thought in a million years that the journey to my God within was by way of my Saddlebred stallion?

Breeders have long bred the best to the best and hoped for the best, but when I finally got the horse I felt was special, he was merely a gift from God. Hours I spent flying on the back of a piece of heaven that helped carry me through what was sometimes living hell. Maybe I wasn't wrong in having everything wrapped up in my horse because his life lifted me up and his death dropped me at the foot of Christ. The loss of my horse was the turning point in my life. I had my "Come to Jesus" moment. Call me crazy, but it has changed my life.

I have my own relationship with God, and I realize how churches and religions can be misguided. And why not, they are just made up of people who mean well but are not perfect. There may be arguments over websites, signs, paint colors or who should or should not be deacons or elders. Interpretations can vary, and any scripture can be taken out of context. But there is no reason to blame God for what people do. We all have a choice to do what is right or to do what is wrong. I realize sometimes people do wrong because they simply don't know how to do right. I find sharing experiences often help others from traveling the same wrong path. I have chosen to tell my own story, and I hope it helps someone avoid the same pitfalls.

Looking back, I realized my greatest sin was the sin of idolatry. I idolized my mother and, probably, my horse. I hitched my wagon to my job, my mom, my church, my husband and my friend. They have all let me down. Or did I let myself down? False idols. God says there will be no idols before me. I thought idols were golden calves or statues of worship, not people or possessions. And money, the whole world seemed to worship that.

No wonder there is so much corruption in the world since money is the root of all evil. If money is the bottom line, why is it on top?

I gave up my old self to embrace the new self. I did not know what was to come or what each day would bring, but I had faith my path would be right. I began to live in the moment instead of tomorrow, next week or the past, and looked to what was in store for me today. Sometimes, I was just amazed at the harmony of creation. For example, as I walked up the road behind my house to the back pasture to feed my horses, the dogs would happily march along. I watched as their pecking order became apparent and I spoke to the leader as she walked along beside me while the others took their place. As I arrived at the little barn, each dog went to their job which they were created to do. I watched the dance. One dog checked for mice and varmints. One kept watch, one was very old and was glad to be alive, while the cattle dog went to work calling the horses to eat. I fed three horses their daily grain, and they picked on each other until they got themselves in a particular order as the dog barked at them. Each day, this procession went on, and as soon as I fed grain, the cattle dog would bark at the horses as I walked away. Then there was silence. I looked back and there she sat, pleased the horses were all in their appropriate places. The next day, the same thing. The next day, she barked one time and quit. I looked back and she sat there pleased. "Good dog." The next day, as I walked off, no barking and the dog trotted past me.

"Lilly, you haven't done your job," I said.

She sat down in front of me and looked as if she had a big grin. I turned around and, to my surprise, the horses were all in their places. I wasn't training them to do any of that. I was observing the harmony of how God's creation worked.

Another day, while working in the farmhouse, the mechanism in the recliner had broken. I needed to take it to the barn to fix it, but I couldn't carry it by myself, and there was no one to help. As soon as I assessed the situation, an older Monte Carlo stopped in my drive and a woman got out and proceeded to walk to my door. She asked if I had a gallon of gas to get her to the station down the street, as her gas tank was empty.

"Of course. It is at the barn. Would you help me carry this chair out to my truck? It needs to go to the barn where the gas is," I said.

She was happy to help me, and I was happy to help her. Whatever I needed--POOF--it was there. I thought about maybe putting goats in the lot behind the farmhouse to clean up some brush. I found myself making an unplanned trip to the landfill at the back of the property and there were two goats wondering in the street. I put them in my pasture to at least keep them safe and eat the brush. I found the owner was my neighbor and she left them there for a while.

I couldn't wait to see what each day brought. I felt as though I walked with God. If I went shopping, there was always a front parking space. Even while visiting my friend in Tennessee, she invited me to dinner at a nice restaurant. "The food is very good, but we may not be able to get a parking space and we'll have to go elsewhere." she said. She drove in and there was a space in front of the door.

"This never happens," she said.

"Welcome to my world. Once I truly found my God, this happens all the time," I replied.

Instead of waking up to what chaos was going to happen, I was intrigued with what wonder would happen that day. It was like being in a whole new world, a new beginning, like being reborn. I had looked quite long and hard about what went wrong in my life, and now I started to observe what was going right. A journey of discovering myself. I liked it.

The Sunday school class has also allowed me to find my voice when I have been disciplined to be quiet. I can speak out on any topic I want, and it has been a place to heal and grow. Other members have thanked me for my informative comments, and I appreciate the opportunity to be heard.

One Sunday, a lady was sitting where I could see her face as she made an excellent point for the first time she spoke. When she finished, she glanced with a look of uncertainty over at me and I gave her a silent thumbs up. She came up to me later and made an even bigger point. "I've been listening to you talk in class and watching the response. You gave me the courage to speak up because in the church I grew up in, women were to remain silent." I agreed with her wholeheartedly.

I was shocked along this journey to discover how religion has been a vehicle to suppress women. I was glad to give up 'walk this way and talk this way' and move into the freedom of being myself.

What I have learned and liked most from my new church is that there is a difference in a relationship with God and religions. I have read the Bible for the first time from cover to cover and have my own interpretation for discussion.

I have found this church to be a restful stop along my healing journey.

Where would I be without the directions given by my friends?

27

My Friends

My good friends gave honest directions to guide me through hard times, anger, and confusion. I was reminded of a joke about the woman on the roof when her house was almost underwater praying to God for help. A man in a rowboat came by and asked if he could help. She said no, she was waiting on God to help. A man in a motorboat came by and asked if he could help. She said no, she was waiting on God. Then a helicopter and she again refused. She drowned. When she got to the Pearly Gates and met Saint Peter, she asked why God didn't help her. Saint Peter replied, "Woman, God sent you two boats and a helicopter!"

I wasn't that stupid! My new and old friends showed up at the right time with what I needed to hear. They helped me solve many issues by taking their time to listen, giving their point of views, and sometimes sharing their own horror stories. Some shared their love stories that ended in traumatic losses of horses, spouses, children, or pets. Others told of their disappointment every Christmas of wanting a horse and never getting it. All were words of comfort because sharing was healing.

I invited a friend to lunch at one of my favorite restaurants in town. My friend had been very supportive to me and had just lost her husband when I was just about to leave mine. She shared her peace after the loss of her husband, as he had said such beautiful things to her his last week on earth. His loving words were bittersweet for me. I was very happy for her peaceful acceptance of her loss, yet tears ran out of the corners of my eyes, wishing my husband could be so sweet to me. She said their relationship was not always peaceful and they had issues too. She said she was the problem, not him. She shared her intense personal buried issue that took years to surface and years to recover. I wouldn't have wanted what happened to me to happen to her any more than she would have wanted me to experience what happened to her. But sharing our stories was what made the difference. After what she went through, I was in awe of the compassionate, strong woman she had become and lucky to call her my friend. I already knew my marriage wasn't the only one struggling and the story of her last days with her husband gave me hope.

Another very close friend was most kind to me. She had just left her husband and farm for a woman. I told her I was glad she found someone to love and continued to support whenever she asked. She eventually returned to her farm and her best friend/husband.

Once I opened up, many more people shared stories. It seemed no one made it through childhood without skinned knees or emotional bruises. A parent left and never came back, or they were terrific but abruptly died. Parents who were impaired could be physically or verbally abusive. I had never imagined sexual abuse by fathers, brothers, uncles, family friends or babysitters. Many people didn't tell family secrets. The stories were endless.

One friend told me how she escaped her husband's murder plot. Her husband and his secret girlfriend plotted to kill her and take her property and life insurance. If it hadn't been for her neighboring girlfriend who clued her in, he might have succeeded. The plot stemmed from her husband's affair with a wrong choice in women. His wife escaped the foiled plot and the gold-digging girlfriend moved on to some other unsuspecting man. Women can be just as evil as men.

Several women told me about abusive divorces. Even men shared this story. All these different sagas just gave me more and more understanding. I was so glad they shared. It was funny, but not funny, how someone else's horror story helped me to see that mine was not so horrible. I suffered from being overly protected, which probably saved me from being physically or sexually abused. I faced my own horror story, determined to heal and forgive, and share my story for good it could do for others.

One friend that I have known since I was ten was always just a phone call away. Any time of the day or many times a day, he would take time to listen to whatever I had to work out. He was a very patient and wise man. Some days, I called him multiple times. I told him just how much I appreciated his time and how much he helped me and asked why would he give so much of his time.

"Don't you remember? Years ago, before you were married, when my marriage blew up and I lost my kids, you were there for me. It was a terrible thing to take a man's children. I was angry enough to think about killing the man who took my wife, but I began to think clearly not let any woman be the reason to spend the rest of my life locked up. If it hadn't been for you, I don't know what I would have done," he said.

My wise friend is glad to return the kindness. He has a warm relationship with his children and grandchildren, and it is very important to him to have them in his life. He is wonderful to help me understand the male point of view in my marriage. He has known my mother for years and like everyone else in the community, respects her. But he thoroughly understands my anger and talking with him has helped me to work through it. His help, in so many ways, is immeasurable. Kindness has great power.

A new friend was a Doctor of Psychology recently employed by the hospital I was committed to so long ago. I became friends with her when we sat together at a lunch outing organized by the church. She said she came from New York to understand why so many people in this area were being committed unnecessarily.

"Well, I'm the poster child for that," I chuckled.

She wanted to hear all about it. I invited her to my farmhouse one afternoon. She sat and attentively listened to my story and never once interrupted. When I emotionally got to the end, she dosed out the best medicine.

"May I hug you?" she asked.

"Of course, you can!" I said, pleased with her response.

She restored my faith in people with credentials because I learned early that some doctors aren't worth the paper their credentials are written on, and some abuse their privileges. I later asked her if she thought I might need to see her professionally.

"No, I would rather be your friend," she said.

We have been so ever since. She gave me the best line of healing from the loss of my former church when she joined our ladies Bible study. One night, we were introducing ourselves and telling a little about ourselves and how we had gotten here. When I spoke of going back to the old church, before I finished my thought, she popped up and said, "No, don't do that, we want you here!" That one statement gave me closure to the entire ordeal. I realized how hurtful it was to be excluded by the group you want.

I invited her to my barn to demonstrate my new technique with horses under the pretext I might want her on my board of directors. During the demonstration I stated this is like Parenting 101.

"How so?" she asked and told about her husband's grandchildren coming to visit that very day. She had no children of her own. With the display of my horse whispering technique, her parenting skill was cooking, and she spiced it up with her own flavor. I saw her at church a week later.

"How was the visit?" I asked.

"It was the best week ever! We had so much fun!" she exclaimed. Love, kindness and know how have great parenting power!

Back at the time when losing my childhood church happened, one of my Kentucky horse friends sent me a picture through Facebook of a man walking away with the quote, "Sometimes the loudest statement you can make is just quietly to walk away." It was great advice. That peaceful solution allowed me, in time, to walk back and visit my childhood church.

My old church friends circled back. It took a while, but one couple, who I dearly loved, called me up and invited me to come back. A year later at a local choral production, the prior preacher was there. We briefly spoke as we passed and afterward when we all were visiting at the end, he slipped up and gave me a heartfelt hug. I was speechless. He didn't say a word and neither did I, but no words were needed. We had stumbled on the key to unlock and open the door to let bitterness escape and understanding and forgiveness slip into our friendship.

Sleep deprivation finally caught up with me and in tears, I called my Psychologist friend for her help. She prescribed a mild sleeping pill. Ah, what a good night's sleep can do for a soul. May I rest in peace with only a pill or two.

What friends can solve as a sounding board. When I screamed out for help, it bounced back in a "trumpet call." The trumpeter, the wife of the pastor, got my attention blowing her horn and drew me into a different church in the first place. The second place I was greeted, by the horn blower, outside the church. I was babbling on about how my world had come crashing down. She listened as I babbled and when I finally shut up, she hugged me. What power a well-timed hug could have.

Sometime later, I asked her if she remembered that day and if she thought I was crazy.

"No, I just thought you had a lot on you," she said.

Later, in her kitchen, she was telling me all she had to do, on and on and on, and she finally shut up.

"Do you think I'm crazy?" she asked.

I thought, "I've seen crazy, and you're not it," and politely smiled.

"You're not crazy," I said. We both chuckled, and she hugged me with great enthusiasm for my support. What great girlfriends!

One day in particular, she was a Godsend. I was sitting in church confiding with another girlfriend about the stress in my marriage. I woke up that morning in tears and I couldn't live like this.

"Is there anywhere you could go to get away and maybe a friend could go with you?" my girlfriend asked.

I told her I had planned a trip to Kentucky to go by myself to pick up a horse. The horn blower overheard me and jumped in like a kid at Christmas.

"KENTUCKY! DID I HEAR YOU ARE GOING TO KENTUCKY? I WENT TO SCHOOL! I LIVED IN KENTUCKY! CAN I GO? OH, I LOVE KENTUCKY! ALL I HAVE BEEN DOING IS COOKING AND CLEANING FOR THE WHOLE FAMILY OVER CHRISTMAS, AND I NEED A BREAK! CAN I GO? OH, I LOVE KENTUCKY!" she said.

The other friend and I looked at each other and knew exactly this was what she had suggested. Sounded like we both needed to escape. In amazement at the timing, I squeaked out a weak "Yeah."

On the trip there as we talked, she discovered and exclaimed, "You have an artist's heart!"

"What's that?" I asked.

"An artist's heart feels more deeply than most every other person and uses their art to interpret those feelings," she said. She taught me something new about myself.

No wonder my heart breaks and pain ran so deep.

A couple of months later, she shared she was going to Florida. I couldn't resist.

"FLORIDA! FLORIDA! OH, I LOVE FLORIDA! I HAVE SOME FRIENDS WHO LIVE DOWN THERE! CAN I GO? OH, I LOVE FLORIDA! CAN I GO!" I exclaimed. It wasn't going to work this time, but my antics were priceless! We laughed, we won. A win-win situation. Life is good.

Her strumming leadership was the reason my son latched onto playing the guitar in the youth band. I wanted to help as it was a chance to spend time with my son away from his dad.

"He doesn't want you here," she said about my son. Was she trying to 'take over' my son?

"He doesn't need to control the world, he needs to learn to **live in it!**" I snapped.

She unintentionally poked a finger in my healing wound of takeovers. I was getting better at dealing with the attempt without a blow up. We got past the encounter like friends should.

She gave me the job of filing her mountain of music. It wasn't exactly the job I wanted, but it did give me a chance to give back to her for teaching my son guitar and be near him, which was what I wanted. I sat in a little room beside the practice room filing, so I could hear my son play more than just occasionally during worship. One morning, she turned practice into a jam session. The guitar player took off and he sounded like Eddie Van Halen or Jimi Hendrix. That was MY SON! I was so happy to experience his performance!

Every Sunday, I filed and filed, yet listened and listened. Finally, one day, the last piece of music was filed. I knew it was time to go because when she couldn't find the sheet music she was using to direct, it was because **I filed it!** My usefulness in this job was over!

I was quite pleased to find out her husband, the pastor, was a horseman too. His message always seemed like it was exactly what I needed to hear. At first, I wondered how this kept happening until I learned when it is your turn to truly hear God, the works like that. I heard the word of God loud and clear.

It took me awhile to place where I had heard the pastor's family name in the local horse circles, but finally, I remembered.

"Did you and your brothers ride in the game races as kids?" I asked the pastor.

"Yes," he answered.

"Were you the pickup man in the rescue race?" I asked.

"Yes," he said with a smile.

I chuckled, "And you ran the race barefooted as I recall."

"Yes," he answered with a bigger smile and maybe a little blush.

How could I not like that?! Not only was he the shepherd of the flock, but a horseman and a cattleman to boot.

His sermons were very motivating and entertaining in his cowboy way. Such as, "…. but that was before I was pasteurized." Or after he broke his ribs from showing off to his friends on an untrained filly, he said to his followers, "It's like my dad says, if you're gonna be stupid, you better be tough." His messages taught many things, including good leadership skills and clarity in following Christ.

He brought the filly over and hired me to help with the job of teaching the horse to be ridden. In less than a week, he and his filly were a picture of trust.

He was so impressed with my ability, he wanted me to give group lessons for the kids who had been riding on his farm, and, he wanted to improve his horsemanship skills over the winter in my indoor arena.

"I like to barter," he said. "I have people who can put lights in your barn."

I thought, "Whoa." This exchange happened **very early** in my anger healing process. My thoughts continued, "Who are your people? Are they your parishioners who think they are serving God when you may be using them to enrich yourself? Isn't that taking the Lord's name in vain? And if your people work for you and pay them, why can't you just pay me? I already told you I have lost everything by losing my career horse. **I need** the money! Are you trying to get my knowledge for free? From what I have gone through to learn what I know, it **ain't for free**! One old farmer friend, years ago, gave me his advice on men. Why **buy** the **cow** if you can get the **milk for free**?

What is it with preachers? One wants his name in lights and the other one wants to be under lights. Hey guys, let me enlighten you. You're not God, just a leader!

My skylights work like I intended; when I don't have enough sense to go home, they put me in the dark. Had I been able to accept the deposit money from the sale of Mark, I was going to use that money to put lights in my barn, **myself!** Everything I do is an irritant to what I have been through. When will this end?"

Please God, could you just stop my brain?

So, I shook my head no and the opportunity fizzled. The most **infuriating** thing about this entire incident was **I couldn't think clearly enough to simply say**, "No, thank you, but I will consider bartering with you for your hay."

Is there anyone **stupider** than a **smart** brunette?!

Ok let's move on.

The relationship with the choir director was the most challenging because she reminded me of the high standards and disciplined ways like my mother.

She and her daughter were best friends like my mom and me. Because of this association, it forced me to deal with my issues instead of filing them away. At times, I would take a vacation from singing in the choir to deal with my inner pain. I only gave my time when I wanted. My mother took my entire life from me twenty-five years ago, and I didn't realize how I had lived under her rule, so I never let my mother's stand-in take anything from me I didn't want to give. It was exercises in regaining my power.

Sometimes I found the quiet solitude on Sundays was a great time to write my book. I used all sorts of exercises to regain my power by using my mother's stand-in. To get in touch with my feelings instead of having "to walk this way and talk this way." Funny, all the different ways I came up with to empower myself. In time I realized I didn't need anyone's permission for what I wanted to do. I quit worrying about trying to share my testimony with only one person when writing it had the potential to reach so many more. I finally found the director more inspirational than frustrating. But sometimes frustration was a great motivator, driving my ability to overcome my fears. I prefer inspiration as it leads to ingenuity which has a more positive feel. Either way, I'm happy to be motivated to create something useful.

During my time in the choir, I had grown to appreciate the ease at which the director could influence many things at once. The piano and organ, the choir, percussion and the orchestra, all accomplished due to the count and tempo. I played flute in the intermediate school band. I sat first chair and it seemed all I did was count. It sometimes felt more like a math class than playing the beauty of music. I had discovered I hate to count! I was happy to leave the counting to the director. Now, I was having fun with the music. A promise fulfilled!

I was entertained at the ease in which the director could cut the music on and cut the music off, make us loud or soft with a variety of arm and hand movements. Finally, with the fun I was promised and delivered with lots of encouragement, they molded me into shape to add to the praise. My tune had changed.

My most treasured new friendship came in the form of a black lady. I asked her if she cared about being called black or did she prefer African American, which has way too many syllables for a Southerner such as myself. It's not that Southerners are slow, we sometimes don't like to waste time. By the time I say A-fri-can A-me-ri-can, I could have a horse saddled up. My friend rattled off a ton of brown colors like caramel, chocolate, brown, mulatto, and many I had never heard referenced in that way before, and she ended with "I don't even know where Africa is." I know that wasn't true because she was highly intelligent, but she didn't refer to her race in the politically correct fashion and apparently it was ok with her I didn't either.

It wasn't just me who took a liking to her, everyone in the church loved her. She was quite open with her way of worship with an added "Amen Preacher" in the middle of a good point. As an excellent choir, we accompanied her with a chuckle and a smile. Everyone instantly loved her "Amen," and we would have said it with her, but we never knew when it was coming.

Our friendship started in a Bible study class she organized. She was suggesting giving up things that unnecessarily take up a woman's time instead of spending it in quiet contemplation with God. The discussion came around to me and it slipped out I gave up my work for a few months. She said, "Goooood." I said, "Well no, not exactly. I quit because..." It was a short version of some of what you have already read, less the commitment story. You could have heard a pin drop in the room. At the end of the night, everyone thanked me for my testimony, and I realized how significant sharing hardships could be. Everyone made it a point to speak to me on their way out. My friend and I were the last ones to leave.

"You know," as I said to my friend, "I grew up middle-class. We didn't live extravagantly, but I had everything I needed and a little more. I had enough clothes, shoes, a bicycle, a horse, a car to go to college and my tuition was paid. And now, I don't care that much about material things. I wear almost the same pair of shoes every day, I carry the same pocketbook until it gets ratty enough a girlfriend tells me I need a new one, and even though my husband and I can buy a new car, I prefer a used one. But do you know what I want most in this world?" She looked at me a little puzzled and shook her head no.

"What I want in this world is **a hug** because my family rarely hugged," I said.

She gave me one of her famous hugs, and I never imagined what that would set off.

She was a much larger woman than I, and when I needed a hug the most, I never saw her coming. POOF! It was as though my big, black guardian angel appeared out of nowhere.

I remember one Sunday morning in a 10' x 10' choir room. There were about five or six white women when I entered, and I had already had a hard morning. My hands were shaking trying to zip up my robe, and as I turned to leave, POOF! there was my perfect timed hug, with a pat on the back and a whisper of "God loves you." WHERE DID SHE COME FROM? I whispered back, "How did you know?" Always, when I needed a friendly hug the most, POOF! she appeared. I never saw her coming. It was truly amazing!

Never in a million years would she have been what I pictured a guardian angel to look like, but I didn't need a picture. She was good. She was like a mom who instinctively knew when a hug was needed. The term "being reborn" was all too real. I felt like a little kid.

I wanted to give back to her for being there for me, and I invited her to my farmhouse for lunch. Our friendship grew and grew, and she shared things about her family and concerns about her grandchildren she was beginning to raise. I spent time with her and her grandchildren any time I had the chance and I specifically made the time. I saw her demonstrate control over her grandson like I have never seen before. I thought long and hard over why she would be like that because I know she loved him deeply. If dysfunction was passed down, it could be traced back. I thought all the way back to slave times. If the young black man didn't do as his master said, the worst punishment that could be done to him was to abuse momma. No wonder a black mother would want to demand her son learn to be controlled. The part of that scenario of which I am most ashamed was that the possible abuse was sometimes carried out, while the white women stood silent, in fear they might lose their position. I will never stand silent on injustice again. Some leaders' ways are not to be followed or respected.

How on earth am I going to explain loosening her control over her grandchildren? I understand very well the desire for freedom and out from under control.

It was several months, and I learned she was leaving for a new job in a new town. On her last day at the church was my only chance to try out my carefully chosen words. I ran out to catch up to her in the parking lot. I was wet with sweat. Could I be quick enough to outrun her, if I triggered her want to hang me out to dry? I always wondered what was meant by the quick or the dead. I hoped that day I wouldn't find out.

"...I know you love your grandchildren very dearly. Good parenting doesn't teach children to be controlled, good parenting teaches them to control themselves," I said.

"But how do you do that?" she asked.

"By consequences. Right now, you can control their world, set the rules, and give them consequences for their actions. When they get out in the world, the same thing is going to happen. They are going to have to pay the consequences if they don't follow the rules. If they don't pay their bills, they lose the item. If they don't follow driving rules, they could lose their license or be involved in an accident. If they get pregnant, that's a biggie. By the time they leave home, you have no control over what they do. It's our job as parents to teach them to prepare for what life brings so they can take care of themselves and their children."

She gave me specific examples and we discussed the solutions. She quickly changed things around for the better for her and her family just because we shared. We were always interested in sharing. With the help of all her friendly hugs, I was able to give back to my guardian angel the positive things my mother had taught me in the form of parenting skills. It helped getting past the bad memories with my mother and the good memories were beginning to come back. My angel and I were right for each other. There has never been a friendship I have enjoyed better than this one reaching across racial lines. I learned black and white women have a lot to teach each other. Again, kindness had great power. And thank God, I chose my words just right.

I decided to push the envelope on choosing words. My carpenter friend and I had built up a lot of trust while working on my farmhouse. He and his wife were sitting beside each other in the front of an overflowing Sunday school class. I wanted to brag to his wife how wonderful her husband was with his work skill. I knew them well enough they could take a joke. Being an attractive woman sometimes creates problems for no good reason. The scene setup with the best opportunity the church had presented me to display what I had learned. I stood directly in front of his wife and leaned in as if to bow to her.

"Thank you for training your husband so well. He does whateeeeever I want," I teased with a giant smile!

Her mouth flew opened as she laughed out loud and quickly started explaining to the other people who heard my colorful remark, while her husband sat grinning like a Cheshire cat. Most men can hardly make **one** woman happy, and I just announced the carpenter's expertise made **two** women happy! How could my compliment be any better?

The next Sunday in the fellowship hall, from the other side of the room his charming wife yelled, "Hey Lisa!" with a giant wave! I was a bright star! I owed it to my charming tone and positively creative choice of words.

Although I had left the stage of showing horses, I found a great platform to enjoy life again, a challenge to learn a new skill and a place to find the courage to face my issues. Performing in harmony with heavenly friends helped me to fly and prepare to launch my new ideas.

X

Arrival At
My Destination of Peace
with Everyone

28

My Rear View Mirror

Glancing back at what is behind me has been a great experience in my life to understand who I am. I have found my voice. I am moving on from the past, from being silenced or erupting with anger into a more harmonious tone, and I continue honing my communication skills. I have moved into peacefully exercising my rights. Instead of juggling the need to please everyone, I have found balance in my life. My ride has left my anger issues far behind.

I traveled a hard road when I stumbled into the darkness of worthlessness and anger. I searched long and hard to find the soft spot, to dig deeper, to uncover buried issues. The further I traveled, I saw that anger was a sign that points to something deep within. It was never about the church sign; it had everything to do with supporting a friend who asked for my help. Nowhere could I find someone to support me when I needed it the most. The amount of money for the website didn't matter, it was about not allowing my work to be taken over and not having someone else's will forced on me. The fear of having someone gain control over me or take away what I have worked for was the root of my defensive actions and anger. I had every right to be angry at the treatment twenty-five years ago, and mad at the attempted takeover of my horse, but it was time to let that anger go. Finding an alternative solution to the church sign wasn't a problem for me. It was that anger issues got in the way of many opportunities. I was my own worst enemy. I wasn't the only one with anger issues.

With so many signs, how can one get so lost?

Amazing Grace came in my view and pulled me in the direction to find myself. I once was lost, but now I'm found, I once was blind, but now I see. I once was deaf, now I do listen, and I once was lame, and now I can stand on my own.

I hold people accountable for their actions rather than take my anger out where it doesn't belong. I will not allow anyone to gain control over me again or take what I am unwilling to give. I can hold someone accountable with a very careful and kind choice of words. My language has finally cleared up. Harsh words, like bullets, bounce off me. It is true life's challenges does make me stronger.

The church sign goes nicely with the architecture of the church. My childhood friend lives at the other end of town in a nicer home away from the church, and the bonds with my special friends are stronger.

Along the way of solving all my buried issues and repairing my relationships, my asthma and allergies have gone by the wayside. I am glad I have lost my diseases. I have found peace inside and out; my mind, heart, body and soul are completely healed.

When I set out on my journey in life, all I have ever wanted to do was to paint pretty pictures and ride pretty horses. I have developed talents in both, gone down wonderful paths and sometimes tripped into a living hell. But after saving myself, all I want to do...is to paint pretty pictures, ride pretty horses and have fun with my family and friends. I have found my brush has broadened and my canvas is larger. I can now paint a picture with words. I have found my calling as an artist, a creator like God, not being God. There is great power in controlling only myself and having influence with others, not power over anyone else.

I have opened my farmhouse as a place for guests and travelers to spend a sometime while visiting and traveling, plus a place for me to renew, be creative, and work with my friends. My mother signed over the deed to my horse farm as part of my inheritance. I am working on my farm developing my new whispering techniques with horses.

I thanked my mother for the gift of my farm and took her out for lunch and a play for her 85th birthday. She quite enjoyed her birthday gift.

"Is this going to be a yearly thing? You know I plan to live to be a hundred," she said.

"OH GOD! NOT THAT!" I exclaimed.

She burst out laughing and then repeated her question. "Well, are we doing this again next year?"

"Well, it depends on what you do to me," I said with a smile. We laughed. We won.

Just the other day, she called me on the phone.

"Ring, ring."

I looked at my phone and thought, "Should I answer this? Ok. I need a little break."

"Hello?" I answered.

"Where are you and what are you doing?" asked Mom.

I thought, "Gosh, she always has to know everything I'm doing. I don't have to tell her, but, why not?"

"I'm at my farmhouse writing," I answered.

"Well, I know how you don't like to be bothered when you are working, BUT THIS IS AN EMERGENCY!" she declared.

"An emergency? This oughta be good. What it is?" I asked.

"Does your lemon pie shake after you cook it for 30 minutes?" Mom asked.

"THAT'S your EMERGENCY?" I replied.

Mom continued, "Well, I need to know..."

There is no relationship quite like what you have with your mother. I hope you have had someone in this life who taught you how to laugh. It is the only way to seriously survive this world. The antics of Lucy and Ethel live on.

Mistakes and difficult situations occur in all families to one degree or another. Some of them are not the least bit funny and sometimes laughter is the best medicine. I hope sharing my story has illustrated that peace, kindness, forgiveness, communication and accountability add up to love. Love does conquer all.

I never liked to fight, nor did I like turning into a roaring lion although it did seem to work. The only reason my fighting worked was that I fought for freedom and peace, not for control or possessions. We all won...or so I thought.

Another fight between my husband and I surfaced. We had a simple misunderstanding and it was about to escalate. I had decided I would never tolerate my husband's harsh words again. Some words don't belong in the world of peace. I had complete control over myself, but would he ever have control over himself? I was simply ready to walk away. I used my words to convey walking away.

"Let's just split this stuff up and go our separate ways," I stated.

My husband came to a lighter tone and soon became quiet. In a short while, he apologized for his words. My words about leaving got his attention. Now that he was listening and had given up fighting, I followed up.

"As hard as I have tried, I cannot protect the children or myself from your sharp tongue. Only **YOU** can control your tongue," I said. He nodded his head, looked at the floor and walked off into another room. He came back and apologized. I graciously accepted his request for forgiveness.

The next day, he was sitting at the table tying a knot in the thread connected to a suture needle. He was using the needle and thread to repair a ham radio project.

"Are you planning on slicing yourself open just to stitch yourself up?" I teased.

"No, I'm thinking about sewing my lips shut to keep me from saying anything stupid," he replied.

"Can I help?" I chuckled.

He laughed. We won. He finally was **aware** and **willing** to control himself! **Touchdown!**

In the end, my husband wanted the same thing I wanted, peace, kindness, and love. We had been fighting for the same goal. I, finally, found someone **as stupid** as a **smart** brunette. We were the **perfect match!**

The other perfect thing in my book is the name of my voice coach, Gay Z., happy to the end. She sings in a positive tone and leads an entire section to happiness. She is my friendly human tuning fork. She pokes me when I'm wrong and is humming when we're right.

Sissie called from Florida asking about our cool plans for the summer. Sisterly love is extremely powerful and cannot be measured. Devil beware, she watches my back.

My son graduated high school with honors and across from the dinner table he says, "Mom, I might want to be a doctor."

Wow. I may have opened up and discovered a doctor. Is **he** the doctor my mother has been talking about? I am so proud. He then wows me by how he can draw with his college laptop. I've discovered our son has an artist's heart like me. The life, I have helped create, is full of surprises. Now, he wants to be a creative illustrator. An artist like me and his dad and a creator like God. **SCORE!**

I am humbled, thankful and blessed.

Thank you, God, for my horse, Mark. For with his life and death, I have found the truth within myself. The golden treasure I have uncovered is my own heart to love, laugh, and live.

29

Dear Mark,

You were never just a horse; you were one special love and together we flew to new heights. I was having the time of my life with you, my mom, and my friends. I was thrown for a loop when the loss of you turned my life upside down. The fall triggered an inside out evaluation to decide what parts of my life were worth keeping. I took a good long look at myself to find my stability.

I dreamed about horses as a child. The mother of my childhood friend, the judge, enhanced my dream of horses when all she talked about was the Bluegrass of Kentucky and Lexington, the horse capital of the world. When it was time to go to college, I knew where I wanted to go, Kentucky. Running with my friends and horses around the Bluegrass of Kentucky was a world of fun.

I learned a lot of lessons in the horse business and some I could have done without, but they were lessons just the same. I dreamed of Kentucky while I lived in Virginia. I worked hard on making my dream come true. When you came along, I knew you were special. As far as I was concerned, I bred, raised, developed, showed, titled, produced offspring with the greatest horse in the world. It was my shortcomings, not yours, that kept us from winning a World Championship title to prove it.

I'm not sure I appreciated what all you meant to me until you were gone. You carried me through, at times, a living hell, and when I needed more power and a lift, you flew me. You were the noblest of God's creatures.

I regret that I did not pick you up immediately after the pre-purchase exam. I feel sure the outcome would have been different. I was looking forward to sitting in the stands eating popcorn and watching your career continue. My friends and family would have joined in to support your rise. We would have done our part to contribute to your win by eating two hotdogs.

I'm glad I allowed the agent and buyers a tryout. You proved to them, on your own, that you were special. Up until the pre-purchase exam, you and I were treated with the utmost respect. After your death, the agent called with heartfelt sympathy and the buyers responded with a card. I feel it would have been a good home for you, as they had the assets and ability to take you to the World Championship Title you deserved.

I did what I could and held the buyer's vet accountable by reporting his unethical behavior to the Kentucky Board of Veterinary Examiners. I promptly received a letter promising dedication to protecting the public. Just like I thought, without the public's help it fell on deaf ears. Like the USA Olympic Women's Gymnastics team, one courageous woman reported the problem years before; deaf ears caused a lot more damage and heartaches. Ethics matter.

I never realized life was such a battle until my trusted and faithful steed died out from under me. It wasn't just a fall; it was a devastating tumble. I was broken, saved, knocked down, suppressed, battered, detached, righted myself, defended my position, showed courage under fire, rose up from the dust, saddled up, stepped in the stirrup to mount yet another courageous and Noble horse and, together, we flagged triumphantly.

Mark, your inspiration lives on.

The Real Ride is a salute to you, my faithful and trusted friend, Mark of Design, the horse that launched me toward freedom and peace. You will always be remembered as the greatest horse in my world.

I have let go. Now you really can fly. You have earned your wings.
I love you so.

Lisa

P.S. I haven't forgotten my promise...

Afterword

So, in conclusion, can you read the signs? Have you heard the road to hell is paved with good intentions? The road to peace is lined with understanding, kindness, and boundaries.

Peace comes from within.

My Grandma Query was right. Family is the most important. All people are children seeking our God; we are a world family. We are a **kind** of Mafia. If you do wrong, you won't be spared and, if you have enough courage to ever save yourself to enter into peace, you won't **want** to get out!

I have enjoyed sharing my story and lessons with you across my kitchen table. A respectable Southern lady always sends family and friends on their way with a couple of treats for the road. I leave you with two such things, in the next few pages, for your journey back home.

And y'all come back, now. Ya hear?

A Family Treat

My family is like every other middle-class family. I do love my family and at some time or another, we have all been a pain to each other. We are a great example of a functional imperfect American family. We all just do the best we can. Funny thing about talking bad about one's family, a member can say anything they want, but if an outsider says anything bad, them they're fightin' words.

I want to tell you of one of my family's most priceless stories which reminds me of a Bible story of two brothers, Esau and Jacob. In the Bible story, the younger brother outsmarts the older brother and tricks him out of his birthright. The trick results in the older brother threatening to kill the younger brother and he must run for his life. It is so common for brothers to fight each other until they have an intruder and then they band together.

In my family's story, the older brother outsmarts the younger brother, and as harmless as all my other stories, results in a great laugh. As children, Mom disciplined us to eat what was good for us and all things in moderation. So, the rule was only one ice cream sandwich per day, same as sodas. Picture Mom, big brother, middle brother and I sitting around the dinner table eating rectangular ice cream sandwiches. My big brother finishes and eyes my brother's sandwich. He knows he can't have another one. With some thought, he begins to instigate his plan.

"Would you like me to make a ball out of your ice cream sandwich?" my big brother asks.

My other brother looks at his ice cream sandwich and with a little encouragement hands the ice cream sandwich over. Mom and I watch the exchange. My big brother very methodically eats the sandwich into a circle and hands the ice cream ball back to him. My mother watches while keeping a straight face.

The next day, even I wanted my ice cream sandwich turned into a ball. How cool! By the third day, my big brother lost interest in taking candy from babies. He knew when to quit and my middle brother and I never knew what hit us. We had learned a new trick...how to eat our own ice cream sandwiches into a ball. And Mom sat there, watched the harmless ingenuity and never said a word. She was the original people whisperer.

Now you see why we all love her so...no matter what she does wrong, the rights outweigh! She never claims to be perfect. As kids, we just want moms to be. And dads too. Perfection not only is impossible, it's boring!!!

Everyone who was invited to our house was always treated as family. We once had exchange students from Italy and Japan. We cooked American food while the Italian cooked his family spaghetti recipe. I had a good time learning the difference in table manners. One showed good manners by slurping his food. One showed it was good manners not to clean his plate. In our family, cleaning the plate showed you like the food. One bathed nightly and the other bathed once a week. I found the differences very interesting. What was "perfect" for one was an insult for the other.

What is perfect anyway? Does anyone really care?

I do care about the foreigner on the train out west who was ready to fight to protect Americans. There is obviously a difference between a good foreigner and a foreign terrorist. Americans and foreigners have more in common than you think. Both want to love and be loved, and both want to escape terrorists. I think foreign terrorists could find something a lot more fun than fighting.

This leads me to answer a previous question earlier in my story: It takes one good humored Pollock and two silly red-blooded American women to wash and show the world how to have fun with a hot-blooded American Saddle Horse's tail! Or is it, one foreigner, two hot women and a hot horse?

Let me paint the picture a little clearer for you. The above scenario sure beats blowing oneself up for forty virgins like your big brother tricks you into believing. I am sure one is smart enough to make a bomb and carry out a plan. But first, let me ask the younger brother some questions:

If your big brother thinks his idea is so great, why doesn't he do it?

If you blow yourself in a million pieces, how could you enjoy even one virgin, let alone forty?

If you kill innocent people, do you think you will end up in the same place as the virgins?

Your journey will be a little like mine. Where you think you are going, is not where you end up. Forty virgins will be in heaven and you will be in hell. You lose, and your big brother wins. I never liked losing a game myself. It is natural for big brothers to want to get the best of little brothers. Don't you think washing a horse's tail with two hot women is a better idea? Or even one woman and who says the lady must be American. Who knows, if you give a lady peace and kindness, plus protection you obviously already know how to do, you might get lucky. You may end up in heaven and not even have to die for it. Bomb making is crazy! Trust me. I've seen crazy!

Learn to ride and groom a horse. Maybe you would end up a bridegroom. Living has so many possibilities!

Maybe if Americans were **kind** enough to ship ice cream and horsemanship into the Middle East, foreigners would have something cool to do besides fight and we all could have some **peace!** Then we could invite foreign tourists to ride horses on a trip west and they would **be happy** to again protect Americans on a train!

Life can be so simple.

And Friends' Treat

I try to make every moment count with my friends. I never know when one may be gone forever. On one occasion, my dressage friends showed me a crazy good time and honed my horsemanship skills, while taking me under their wing at the World Equestrian Games, hosted in The Kentucky Horse Park in Lexington, Kentucky. We ended up in the Champagne tent with the winner, horse owner and team members the night after the event. The winning horse owner came up beside me while ordering glasses of champagne. Since I like to make friends, I couldn't resist the temptation. This was too easy. I struck up a conversation and I found him to be a delightful man. He bragged about his horse like every other horse owner I knew but the difference was, not only had he earned bragging rights, the rumored worth of his horse was well into the millions of dollars! At the end of a most delightful conversation, he handed my friend and me each a glass of champagne. That was some very unexpected and entertaining fun!

I would like to repay my fun-loving dressage friends with one of the greatest stories passed around the showgrounds for many years with my fun-loving Saddlebred friends.

To tell the most entertaining story, I must go back to when I was living in Kentucky working horses with my boss. Even though my boss sometimes gave me a hard time, lots of times we had great fun. This was one of those times. He wanted me to meet the queen of the Saddlebred world at the time.

I called her 'the queen' because during her Saddlebred reign, she bred, bought and developed countless World Champions. She acquired the top who's who list of clients and even brought in Hollywood royalty. In addition, she thought outside the box with her idea and execution to syndicate a stallion for a million dollars, a first-time figure in the Saddlebred world. After there was nothing more to do in our horse world, she moved on to the thoroughbred racing world. I didn't follow her career in the racing industry, but she obviously had an eye for a good horse. She was a shrewd business woman.

My boss made an appointment with 'the queen' and we drove to her farm. She graciously invited us in her lovely home. While my boss and she talked, I admired a painting by one of my favorite equine artists. The oil painting depicted she and her husband, each riding a champion in the show ring together. On the other wall was a trophy cabinet loaded with large silver trophies. I politely asked her if I could inspect them more closely.

"Of course," she said. I knew I was standing in the middle of a rare lifetime experience.

"No one can ever take away what you know," was her advice to me that day.

My boss couldn't wait to tease 'the queen' about the time she caught her husband in, I guess I would say, a compromising position with another woman. The queen didn't waste any time going to find her gun and loading. Her husband knew his wife quite well and he wasted no time running out the end of the barn, as he was frantically trying to save his hide.

BANG! She shot!

Bullets hit around the door as he ran out! She reloaded and went after him.

BANG! as she hit the tree he was hiding behind!

BANG! as she hit the next tree he took shelter behind!

There was no safe place he could hide! He knew he had only one way out! If he could run fast enough to make it to the broodmare field, he would be safe!

BANG! As she hit the tree he ran past!

His safety depended on the fact, he knew, she would never shoot one of her broodmares! His calculation allowed him to live to see many more days. Not with her, but she let him live!

My boss's question to 'the queen' was this, "Did you really mean to shoot him?" as he laughed.

"I hit everything I meant too," she replied. What a crack shot! Move over Annie Oakley.

Now, I knew where her advice originated.

My boss was having the time of his life teasing her while trying to impress me. As hard as he ribbed her, she wasn't the least bit ruffled. I hoped it stayed that way.

I will never forget the day my boss entertained me visiting with 'the queen.' My boss wasn't all bad. Actually, he could be quite fun. He taught me many useful lessons and I enjoyed the lessons I learned from 'the queen' of the Saddle horse business. The advice, "No one could take away what you know," in time, became very important to me. She gave me a lesson on picking broodmares that day and she demonstrated another universal lesson: Hell hath no fury like a woman scorned! A consequence that could have been avoided if Thou did not commit adultery.

And speaking of unintended consequences. Do you really think it is a good idea to sell guns to women, teach them to shoot and give them a conceal carry permit? Do you think maybe you should be very careful about ruffling females' feathers? Or should I say, wake a sleeping lion?

A lot of women have had enough. Has yours?

If you think arming the teachers is a smart idea, go ahead, women have a right to bare arms. They can just shoot the boys they know to be problems. The fruit doesn't fall very far from the tree. This could be double action: teachers could aim to save more lives and save future wives a lot of headaches at the same time.

I don't think any of part of this short story is a very good idea, except enjoying friends, but what does it matter what I think? All along, I've been thinking there's nothing STUPIDER than a SMART brunette!

Author

Lisa Worrell-Whittle is an artist, author and accomplished horsewoman. Born and raised in the Blue Ridge Mountains, Lisa lives in Galax, Virginia, with her husband and their son is college bound. She continues to breed and develop beautiful Saddle Horses in Hillsville, where she owns Mark of Design Farm and Farm House Retreat and Mark of Design Publishing, Subsidiaries of Mark of Design, LLC.

The Real Ride is her first book.

Email therealridebook@gmail.com to add your name to the author's list. We will notify you of future releases.

To purchase a copy or copies of the book or eBook, go to Www.markofdesignllc.com